THE RV
PASSIVE INCOME
GUIDE

Learn The Laptop Lifestyle And Swap Your
Day Job For Full-Time RV Living

JEREMY FROST

ISBN: 978-1-989635-30-8

CONTENTS

Formal education will make you a living;
self-education will make you a fortune.

– *Jim Rohn*

INTRODUCTION

WHEN WAS THE last time you truly felt free? Free to jump in your RV and go see all of the places that you have always wanted to see?

I'm going to guess that right now you are stuck in the 9-5 grind, desperately wanting to downsize your life, purchase and move into your dream RV, and go experience all of those places on your bucket list that you have only ever seen other people travel to. Or, perhaps, you already own your dream RV but can only travel as far as a weekend will take you.

There is one big problem staring you in the face - your travel options are drastically limited because you have to return to your soul-sucking job every week on Monday. Then you spend the next five days dreaming about taking your next RV trip, only to be left obsessing about having to go back to work on Monday again.

Let's face it - traveling takes money. Even if you have a good chunk of change saved up, you are still going to need to pay bills, like your cell phone and insurance. Your savings can get eaten up really fast if you consistently have money going out and nothing coming back into your savings or checking account.

Even if you are downsizing, you still have to consider expenses like gas, food, insurance, parking, and activities - unless you only ever plan on parking in the WalMart parking lot. You want to quit your job and go on the road traveling in your RV, living the lifestyle that you see all over social media. But in order to quit your job and live your dream life, you need to find a way to make money while you are traveling in your RV.

Or win the lottery, but let's not count on that...

You might have heard stories about how people have made great money online and are now able to travel full time. It seems like every time you scroll through Instagram, you see new posts about someone traveling full time. But is that really something that YOU can do?

Without a doubt...YES!

It is possible to make a very good income online without having to sacrifice the best hours of the day. The best part is that you can even make some really great passive income so you can actually enjoy your time traveling and not be stuck at a computer all day long, because there is no point in living in an RV full-time if you can't actually go anywhere or do anything!

This guide is going to teach you everything a beginner needs to know to get started making money online so you can live your laptop lifestyle, quit your time-consuming day job, and join the ranks of full-time RV living!

In this book, you are going to learn a variety of ways to earn income online that will continue to pay you well into the future. Each chapter reviews a different business model where you will get actionable steps on how to proceed with each business so you will have success from the start rather than trying to reinvent the wheel.

Starting an online business can be scary - especially if you have never done anything like it before - but it doesn't have to be. Once you are armed with the knowledge of how to start an online business, you can tackle your new adventure with confidence and excitement every day.

But why the heck should you listen to some guy you have never met before?

Hi, I'm Jeremy Frost!

Although I have been a full-time RVer for over five years, which I spoke about in my previous book *The RV Lifestyle Manual*, many people don't realize that I started my journey with little savings and just a laptop. My interest in online business started many years before I hit the open road with my RV and although I didn't plan it at the time, these two things created the perfect marriage for me to live out my dream lifestyle.

And you can do it too!

In this book, I'm going to give you all the essentials that took me years of failure and persistence to learn how to be successful.

Your time on this planet is limited, and there is no reason you shouldn't be doing what you love. Stop just settling and living your life to make someone else money.

Go see the world, have new experiences, wake up every day with a sense of purpose and passion. You aren't in this world to just work, pay taxes, and die. This guide is going to give you the tools you need to start living your best life, on your own terms!

But I must warn you...

This isn't one of those get rich quick schemes, pyramid schemes, or multi-level marketing buy-ins, and you won't be trying to push weight loss pills and powders to your friends and family on your social media profiles.

I am talking about creating a real, sustainable business with products and or services that will not only help people but will continue to pay you for years to come while doing something you actually enjoy and are passionate about. Real businesses take time, effort, and planning. What I'm going to show you in this book is that building a real business is a lot less complicated than you might think.

Once your business is generating a real and sustainable income, you will be able to travel, not ever have to worry about waking up to that annoying alarm clock (if you don't want to), or just hang out with your friends, all while your business is making money for you. That is if you are doing this correctly. The power to live the lifestyle you want is in creating systems and processes that generate passive income.

Over the last several years, I have helped fellow full-time RVers make passive income online, and it has dramatically changed their lives for the better. Not to brag, but I can't tell you how many thank you emails and praise I have received from helping other people learn to make passive income online so that they can live their best lives. Heck, I even get the occasional snail mail in my P.O. Box here and there. I love the feeling of helping others achieve their dreams and break out of a life they think they have to live because that is what society tells them they have to do!

I hope to be able to spread this passive income guide throughout the RV community and be able to help thousands of more people each and every year.

While I wish that everyone who reads this book can create a business that earns them six-figures per year, like myself, I can't guarantee how much you will make. It all depends on your ability to take consistent action and implement the things you learn in this book. It's unfortunate, but many of you will read this book, get excited about building a business, but never actually do it!

What I can promise you is if you take action right now, you will earn your first dollar of passive income online within 30 days of finishing this book. It might only be enough for a small coffee, or you might make enough to cover your bills for the next month, it all comes down to how much effort you are willing to put into your business.

Think about it, if you can make your first dollar (or more) in a month from now, what can you do in three months, then six months? How badly do you want to hand in your resignation at work and pack up your RV without having a set date that you need to come back?

This guide is going to show the differences between earned income and passive income while dispelling some of the myths of each. Then we will cover the passive income models that have been proven to work for me, *Jeremy Frost*, and make me six-figures a year consistently.

We all already know that we live in a technology era. Many of the best opportunities to earn substantial passive income are wide open right now. Gone are the days of having to invest huge chunks of money into real estate to be able to generate a passive income. There is lots of money to be made, a low barrier to entry, and much less competition. This is only going to change in the future as things will become more competitive, and people start to embrace the laptop lifestyle and realize that they don't have to work 9-5 anymore.

So you could read this book, think *"oh that's nice for him, he probably had some special advantage, blah blah, blah"* and do nothing.

OR...

You can read this book and take the necessary steps to start building your laptop lifestyle so you can quit your day job and live the full-time RV life.

The time is now! Take action on what you learn in this book and set yourself up for success and financial freedom for the rest of your life. Travel the world in your RV, spend time with your friends and family, and make new memories. I'm going to show you how I've done all of this and more by earning a passive income online, and you can do it too!

So let's get started!

CHAPTER ONE
What Exactly Is Passive Income And How You Can Use It To Your Advantage

YOU MIGHT THINK that passive income is only for those that are already wealthy - multi-millionaires with portfolios of hundreds of thousands of real estate holdings and such. While many people who are already wealthy have several streams of passive income, it is not some big secret and exclusive thing that only those "in the know" understand how to do.

Did you know that the average millionaire has seven different streams of income?

I'm going to let you in on a little secret "they" don't want you to know about...

ANYONE CAN CREATE PASSIVE INCOME!

There, the cat's out of the bag.

It doesn't matter if you were born into money or are living paycheck to paycheck. With a little bit of knowledge and a lot of hard work, anyone can create a business that generates passive income.

In this chapter, we are going to cover the difference between active and passive income, how you can prime your mindset for success, and why trying to be perfect is the wrong thing to do. I will also dispel some of the myths of passive income and how to avoid shiny object syndrome.

ACTIVE INCOME VERSUS PASSIVE INCOME: WHAT YOU NEED TO KNOW

But what's the difference between passive income and just regular old (otherwise known as active) income?

Active income is when you go to your job, put in your hours, and get paid. You have to be ACTIVELY working to earn the income and it is generally an hourly wage or a salary. You call in sick...you don't get paid. You get fired, then you really don't get paid.

Passive income is income that you earn that "requires little to no daily effort to maintain," (Hogan, 2019). Passive income is not just something where you flip a switch or click a few links and you are generating thousands of dollars per day. If someone promises you this, run far away, it is a scam!

Passive income is actually built by putting in a lot of effort in the beginning to build something that then makes you money even when you are not working on it. Heck, it can even make you money while you sleep! Imagine, when you are generating passive income, log into your bank account and it has increased, without you doing any additional work! It really is an amazing feeling.

There are many benefits to creating a passive income, beyond just being able to travel when and where you want in your RV. Passive income helps to build wealth, gives you the ability to retire early (or start RVing sooner), provides protection in the case that you would lose your primary source of income, and provides you with additional income if you outlive your retirement funds.

The primary benefit of passive income in the RV lifestyle is that you can travel, make money, and not have to worry about working all the time. You get to actually enjoy your life and your travels.

You are not going to become a millionaire overnight with passive income (if it were that easy, everyone would do it!). You can, however, build up some serious streams of income over the long run.

Depending on what kind of business (or businesses) you are building, passive income can mean a few thousand dollars a month to hundreds of thousands of dollars...PER MONTH!

Now, I know that might sound crazy at this point, especially if you haven't even made your first dollar online. But believe me, it is completely achievable. Once you start seeing what is really possible, it becomes real and not just a dream anymore.

There are literally tons of ways to create passive income online. The ones that we are going to address in this book are self-publishing, freelancing, blogging, YouTube, affiliate marketing, Amazon FBA, and selling your business for a big payday.

You might also consider if you already own a home and are going to be traveling in your RV full-time, renting out your home for passive income each month. Look at other comparable rental properties in your area, how much do you think you could charge? What is your current mortgage? While this is not a topic that we cover in this book, it is something to take into consideration.

THE SUCCESS MINDSET AND HOW TO ACHIEVE IT

The first step in building your business is getting your mindset right. Your mindset has more to do with your success then you realize.

There is one thing that successful people realize that many others do not - time is their most valuable asset. If you want to truly build wealth, you have to value your time more than you value money. When it comes to making money online many people have this instant gratification mindset. They want to make money yesterday. They aren't willing to plant their tree for the future.

You need to be willing to sacrifice for a while before you start making a steady income.

Your mindset is so important when it comes to building your business. You can have the most amazing website, write the best book, follow all the right marketing strategies, but if your mindset isn't right, then you aren't going to reach your full entre-preneurial potential.

Perhaps you think that you weren't meant to be an entrepreneur. Get that out of your head right now! If you have the passion, the drive, the knowledge, and are willing to work for it, then you ARE meant to be an entrepreneur! There are so many successful entrepreneurs that started their own businesses after being fired from their jobs.

There is a reason you picked up this book, there is a reason you were drawn to earning income online so that you can travel in your RV full time and live your best life. People who are not meant to be entrepreneurs don't read about this kind of stuff. They are happy working their 9-5 jobs and never looking for anything different.

Remember when you were young and your mother told you that you could be anything you wanted to be when you grew up? She wasn't lying. As we get older our mindsets change from playing make-believe that we are explorers and letting our imaginations run wild. The reality of paying bills and working for someone else smacks you in the face and your dreams slowly die. But it doesn't have to be that way! You can be an entrepreneur, you can live your best life, and travel the world on your own terms.

You also have to keep in mind that to fail is part of the process. You learn a lot from your mistakes and from your failures. Your journey into entrepreneurship is not going to be perfect. The process of becoming an entrepreneur and building your business is just as important as the end product of the passive income you will make. Don't worry about doing everything perfect, worry about your progress.

Perfection is the enemy of progress

It is better to get your website up and running, even if you think it's ugly, even if it's not fully optimized. Making something and putting it out into the world is going to get you to your goal faster than if you don't do anything until it's perfect.

With the mindset of not being good enough, you also might think that you are too late to jump on this online income bandwagon. This is simply not true! You actually have a huge advantage to starting later, you learn from other people's mistakes, find loopholes, and scope out your competition. While you might think competition is a bad thing, it's not. Having competition in your market means that there is a need for your business.

Don't fall into the trap of making excuses not to get started. You are never too old and it is never too late. The best time to start your business is now with what you already have! There is no magical "right" time to get started.

Don't go at it alone

Just because you are going to be using the internet to make your income doesn't mean that you should be doing it alone. In fact, you shouldn't be doing it alone at all! While being an entrepreneur can be lonely, you should make it a point to connect with others that are in a similar situation and build relationships.

Perhaps there is someone that you found online that is where you would like to be in a year or two, reach out to them. Generally speaking, entrepreneurs love helping one another. If you don't want to reach out to someone individually, try attending a conference where you can meet people that are doing the same type of thing you are doing. This is a great opportunity to connect with other entrepreneurs and industry leaders.

There are hundreds of conventions held throughout the world every year for business owners and entrepreneurs of all kinds. You can also find local meetups in your area for entrepreneurs. Meet people any way you can, create connections, and build relationships.

There is one core thing to remember with this though, always give before you take. Don't email someone saying how much you admire them and off the bat ask them to mentor you for free; you likely won't get a great response. If you really want to be mentored by someone, then you need to establish a relationship with them first.

Work on your mindset every day. It is like a muscle, you can train it to work for you. Say positive affirmations about your business rather than saying negative things that will steer your mindset in a negative direction.

DISPELLING THE MYTHS AND LIES ABOUT PASSIVE INCOME

Just as with everything else online, there are many myths around passive income. Here we are going to go over some of the most common myths related to passive income.

The set it and forget it method

There is no set it and forget it method that is going to generate you hundreds of dollars a day. While there are a ton of "programs" online that tout they have the answer to 100% passive income where you push a few buttons and you will be generating millions of dollars online without ANY work, these are straight-up scams. They take advantage of people that are unfamiliar with the online business space. Do not EVER sign up for anything that promises these types of claims.

Real income takes real work.

Even things like real estate investing and websites you need to check in on once in a while to make sure they are still working and doing what you want them to do, all still require work. Unfortunately, there is no such thing as 100% hands-off, passive income. You can, however, invest time upfront to get everything up and running then check on things periodically to make sure everything is still generating you the money you want without sucking up all of your time and energy. Or you can hire someone to run it for you.

You can set it up quickly

The goal of passive income is to be able to not only generate you money but also give you time freedom. While it does take a lot of time and energy to get your passive income streams initially set up, once everything is up and running you shouldn't have to put as much time and effort into building the business. Instead, more of your efforts will go into sustaining it. Once the business is built you can find ways to automate things through software and outsourcing as we've already discussed.

Remember

Creating passive income has just as much to do with your mindset, as we discussed before, then it does with your knowledge and hard work. Some people don't believe what you think really matters, but what you think is what becomes your reality. If you think you aren't cut out to be an entrepreneur, then you aren't. If you think that you can create streams of passive income to live your best life traveling in your RV, then that is what is going to happen. Squash those limiting beliefs and get your mindset right before anything else.

You only need one good income source

Remember earlier when I said that on average millionaires have seven different income streams? Well, if they are already millionaires, there is a reason they have multiple income streams. Think about this, if the only way you generate revenue is with your job, what happens when you get fired? No more revenue. The same goes for building a business. Say you publish a book, one book, and it does really well and that is your only revenue stream. Suddenly, something happens, your book gets blacklisted, banned by Amazon and all major retailers. You are out of income!

This is why millionaires generate multiple passive income streams - to stay millionaires.

You need money to make money

There is a really big misconception that you need to invest thousands of dollars in order to get started making money online. The people who are making you believe that are the ones making money from selling thousand-dollar courses on how to make money online.

Do you see the trend there?

You can start a self-hosted blog (more on that in Chapter Four) for less than $100. You can publish a book on Amazon or start freelancing for literally nothing.

While you are going to need a lot more capital if you are planning on investing in real estate, it is possible to start an online business for $0!

CHOOSING A BUSINESS MODEL: HOW TO AVOID SHINY OBJECT SYNDROME

Starting an online business can lead you down one giant rabbit hole. The more you learn about creating a business online, the more you want to learn about it, and there are millions of programs you can buy, coaches you can work with, and businesses that you can try.

But that is not the goal here. The goal is to choose a business model that will work for you and stick with it. Now you can certainly create other businesses in the future, but only after you have one that is successful and that is generating you income.

Back to the whole instant gratification thing...

People are impatient. When they want something, they want it now, and having a successful business is no different. You can't expect to open your virtual doors and have people flooding through with credit cards in hand. It just doesn't work that way. You have to be willing to put in the work and wait to reap the long-term rewards.

Your online business is not *Field of Dreams,* no one is going to come because you built it.

When you decide to open an online business there are going to be challenges, believe me! Success is not a straight line, there are hills, potholes, rivers to cross, and mountains to climb. Don't give up when you come to that river. Instead, fall in, build a bridge, then cross it. There are going to be plenty of times where you think to yourself, *"What am I doing?! Why am I doing this?!,"* but don't give up too soon. There is a famous quote by Thomas Edison, *"I didn't fail, I just found 10,000 ways it didn't work."*

It is very exciting when you first start your business and everything is new. However, over time that excitement will wear off and you might want to say forget it and move onto something else, maybe something that you think is going to be easier or more fun or make you more money. As an entrepreneur, it is very easy to get distracted by shiny objects and never really, fully commit to your business. What many people don't realize is that the newest tactic is not what moves the needle on your business, it is the core fundamentals that keep you moving forward in your business.

If you dabble in your business you are never going to get very far. Whichever path you choose, you should go all in, become a master of your business niche. Invest in yourself and your business in things that will bring you - and your customers - value.

You are going to need to abandon short-term thinking and start to think long-term. It's going to take a lot of work and you might not see the results you want for months or even longer. Get rid of your distractions - instead of sitting down and watching TV at night, work on building your business. You don't need to start from scratch, there are plenty of resources online to help you get started. While there are many great, free resources available, don't be afraid to invest in yourself. Although make sure you do your research before you buy any program or course to make sure that the person selling it isn't just there to take your money and run.

You truly have unlimited potential inside of you, don't waste it!

CHAPTER SUMMARY

Passive income is income that you receive for work that you have previously done. Active income is where you have to be actively working in order to get paid (like a regular 9-5 job).

Anyone can create passive income streams. You don't have to already be rich and hire a team to start generating passive income. Passive income takes work to establish, more so in the beginning and not so much on a daily basis once you have it set up.

There is no such thing as flipping a switch and clicking a few links to generate passive income, these are scams!

There are many benefits to passive income:

- Financial freedom
- Additional protection

- Can create multiple streams
- Time freedom

Before you decide on what type of business you are going to build, you need to get your mind right first. Mindset is everything when it comes to building a business. If you believe you will succeed, then you will. If you have a negative mindset that you are never going to make it, then that is exactly what is going to happen.

Building passive income is like planting a money tree for the future. It's not going to bloom overnight, it's going to take time. The wealthy realize that time is more valuable than money and build their businesses accordingly. Don't let your imagination and your dreams die.

Don't try and be perfect. You are going to make mistakes and you are going to fail. That is part of the process. I have never met another entrepreneur that hasn't failed and made mistakes. The important thing is that you learn from them and don't get discouraged.

Learn from other people's mistakes as well. Having a bit of competition is a good thing, it means that there is a demand to be fulfilled.

Stop waiting for the right time and just start now!

Connect with other entrepreneurs through meetups, conferences, and conventions. Build relationships with others in your space. If you blog, reach out to other bloggers, and so forth.

There is no set and forget method to passive income, period. Don't believe anyone who says otherwise, they are just going to take your money and run.

It is going to take time and effort to actually start to generate passive income. It is also in your best interest to generate multiple streams of passive income so you never have to worry about having to go back to your job because you lost your one stream of passive income. You also don't need a huge monetary investment to get started. Just your time and a lot of work.

Do your best to avoid shiny object syndrome and focus on one main business to start with rather than being all over the place. This will make growing your business a lot easier. Don't give up too soon, keep your head up, even when you feel like you might be failing. There are going to be challenges and you need to rise above them. Stick to the core fundamentals to keep your business growing.

Tap into your potential and get started!

In the next chapter, we are going to cover all about how you can get started making your first dollar online, even if you have never previously made money online or operated a business in your life.

CHAPTER TWO
How To Earn A Great Income As A Freelancer

Although people don't often view freelancing as your typical passive income work, it is the fastest and most effective way to make your first dollar online. Rather than having to build a whole business from scratch and learn a new skill set, you can use the skills you already have to start building an income. You can then reinvest that income into another business that will allow you more passive opportunities.

Often times, making your first dollar online has nothing to do with your skill set but rather your mindset. If you have never owned a business or made money outside of your normal job, then you have been stuck in an employee mindset. Having an employee mindset is not going to get you to your passive income goals. While freelancing is not going

27

to make you millions in your sleep, it is a great way to get your foot in the door and start to learn about the ins and outs of making money online.

You probably already have some skills that you don't even realize that you can use to become a freelancer. So keep reading to find out how you can start your first online business with nothing but your knowledge, a computer, and a lot of hard work and determination.

There are so many great things about freelancing and living the RV life! For starters, you get to pick your own hours, how much work you take on, and which clients you work with. With freelancing, you can take on as much or as little work as you like. Want to visit a more expensive location? Take on another client project or two to fund your fun!

In this chapter, we are going to cover how to make your first dollar online as a freelancer, what you can freelance, what the best platforms are for freelancers, if freelancing can actually be passive, and how and why you should reinvest your earned income.

HOW TO MAKE YOUR FIRST DOLLAR ONLINE

There are millions of freelancers online doing a wide variety of various jobs and tasks to earn income. Some even earn a rather substantial income from freelancing, but it's not easy. Building your presence and your client base online takes a lot of work and dedication. However, once you have a good client base built up, it can be pretty easy to get repeat business and a reliable income every month.

I would like to first address the differences between a freelance job versus a gig or contract worker. Freelancers can be hired on just like a regular employee or on a contract basis. There are advantages and disadvantages to each.

Freelance employee

Being hired as a freelance worker to a company gives you the freedom to work from anywhere your RV takes you (as long as there is WiFi). Many of the freelance positions available offer time flexibility as well, meaning you don't have to be "clocked in" at certain times. You might, however, have to attend team meetings at certain times. Just make sure you are getting your time zone conversions correct! Being employed as a freelancer can also provide the benefit of health care insurance, paid time off, and other employee type benefits. You also benefit from consistent work, either for clients or for the company itself.

The major disadvantage is that you are still working for someone. You might have to take on clients that you don't want to work for or don't really like. Depending on the position, you might not have too much time flexibility as well. It varies from company to company.

Independent freelancer

Working gigs or being a contract employee can allow you a bit more freedom but also comes with its own set of challenges. If you choose to go out on your own, you are going to need to build your own client base, which can take time. The great thing about this is you get to choose who you work for and what you are charging. You don't have to worry about reporting to anyone other than your clients and can work when and where you want to.

The biggest disadvantage to this is that you don't get any kind of employee benefits. While this can be hard for some people to swallow, especially if you have always been used to having health insurance through an employer, there are options. You can check out the self-employment section of HealthCare.Gov or see if your home state offers some type of state insurance for self-employed people.

Once you have determined which type of freelancing you would like to do and you have an idea of what skills you are going to be using, it's time to start on your search for clients and making that first dollar online.

WHAT KIND OF FREELANCING CAN YOU DO?

There are literally hundreds of different freelancing jobs and gigs available to do online. Here is a list to get you thinking about some of the freelance jobs that you could do:

- Voiceover artist
- Writer/copywriter/ghostwriter/blogger
- Web designer
- Graphic designer
- Virtual assistant
- Social media manager
- Translation
- Transcription
- Illustration
- Video editor
- Songwriter
- Game development

- Mobile app development
- Ecommerce
- Consulting
- Greeting card designer
- Data Entry
- SEO specialist

And that is just a few off the top of my head! While you can certainly learn just about any skill needed for these freelancing positions, there are a few things to keep in mind. You should have an interest in doing this long term and be good at it. You don't want to have just another job, that would kind of defeat the purpose of freelancing to live the RV life. You also want to be sure that you are good at what you do. If you aren't good, it's not likely that you will get repeat customers and referrals for new business.

If your 9-5 is something that you could turn into a freelancing gig that is a great place to start. Perhaps you currently do data entry, or manage your company's social media, use this experience as a starting point. You can always pivot later as your goals change and as you build up a client base.

One of the great things about having a client base is that you can cross-sell or up-sell them on different services. Perhaps you are a freelance writer who has learned how to do social media management. You can cross-sell your services for additional revenue streams.

WHAT ARE THE BEST PLATFORMS FOR FREELANCERS?

There are tons of different freelance platforms online that you can start on. Some of them have a very low barrier to entry, while others take some time to build up a reputation and client base before you can start to get work that actually pays well.

Upwork

Upwork is, in my opinion, one of the best and biggest platforms for freelancers out there. You can find freelance work in everything from web design to customer service. Not only are there many types of freelance work available on Upwork, they make signing up and managing your gigs super easy. As with many other platforms, the more you work on Upwork, the better reviews you get, and the more easily you can find work there. Make sure that you are creating a freelancer profile that really showcases your skills and talents while creating stellar proposals to send to clients. Upwork even offers an app that makes connecting with clients super simple and easy to keep everything organized. Furthermore, the more work you can get through Upwork, the less you will have to pay in fees, so that's a win-win!

Facebook

If you are just starting, look to Facebook. There are thousands of Facebook groups for every kind of freelancing work, as well as general groups. It might take a bit to find one that you like, and that has legit opportunities, but it can be a great place to start. Many of the people in the groups are looking for help within their own businesses and want to help other business owners (that's you, the freelance business owner).

Simply start your Facebook search by typing in relevant keywords in the search bar, such as "writer," "freelance," or "web design," and see what comes up for groups. Join as many groups as you can to get started with, then work your way through the groups to see which ones are going to be the most beneficial to you.

Fiverr

Fiverr is another great place for freelancers to get started. There is a very low barrier to entry, and if you know what you are doing and can create some recurring clients, you can earn a good income. The basic concept of Fiverr was born on creating a service-based business where entrepreneurs and businesses could get help on things like writing blog posts and getting a logo designed for as little as $5.

But fear not, you don't have to worry about just working gigs for $5 each, you can make a lot more on Fiverr! People can make up to $10,000 per transaction on Fiverr (based on their services and experience, of course!).

Working with clients

There are a few things to keep in mind when you start looking for work on freelance platforms. You have to be good and actually know what you are doing! On many freelancer platforms, you get new clients based on your previous reviews. If you have a bad review, you aren't likely to get new clients.

While many communications happen over messaging and email, you might have to TALK to a potential client in order to sell them. When this happens, you have to be sure that you can sell your services when talking to someone. You aren't going to get clients if you don't have a clear message that you are communicating to them and letting them know what you can offer them.

You also need to know your minimum rate and not have to worry about competing against someone who is only charging $5 for their services. There are many different ways to calculate your rate, but make sure to factor in the fees that the freelance platform takes out.

While you might think that it is difficult to compete against someone overseas who is charging only a fraction of what you charge, there is one very large factor that business owners are willing to pay for, and that is quality. A higher-quality product can be produced when both parties fully understand each other. It is not to say that business owners should discount working with someone overseas, but there are many people that prefer to work with someone who is in their region.

You should also be aware of your competitors' prices and why you can charge more. If you are based in the US, you will tend to have an advantage for business owners that are looking to outsource to US freelancers. Once you have some great reviews under your belt, you can certainly start to raise your rates. But don't forget to be realistic here, you can't completely rely on freelance platforms for your income. You are going to need to build up a client base outside of the platforms just like with any other online position. As the old saying goes, you can't put all of your eggs in one basket. You need to diversify and make sure that you are moving towards being able to be in full control of your clients and your income. At any point anything that is a platform can delete all of your information and all the information you have on your clients, then you are left with nothing.

Other freelancer platforms include:

- UpWork (already discussed above)
- Fiverr
- Freelancer
- Envato Studio
- PeoplePerHour-Great for those located in the UK
- TopTal-Great if you are already an expert in your field

You can also look for freelance and remote positions on job board sites as well. Many remote jobs offered on job boards offer plenty of location independence, and you can also find contract and freelance positions rather than traditional "jobs." Freelance writing is very popular to start out with, and there is certainly no shortage of work available.

Some great job boards to start on are:

- Problogger
- ZipRecruiter
- Indeed
- Glassdoor
- LinkedIn
- SmashingJobs
- BloggingPro
- MediaBistro
- SoloGig
- JournalismJobs
- WeWorkRemotely
- Online Writing Jobs
- Freelance Writing
- All Freelance Writing

Use search terms like "remote," "virtual," or "work from home" to search for location-independent positions.

Can freelancing be passive?

This can be a difficult question to answer. While the goal of living the RV lifestyle is to create passive income so that you can spend your time driving to and enjoying destinations that you have always dreamed of, you still have to be able to make money to fund your new lifestyle. But let's face it, if you are spending 8-10 hours a day working (or looking for new work) that doesn't leave you much time to enjoy your new RV lifestyle.

So, no freelancing can not be passive - at least in the beginning. The catch 22 here is that you need to build up a client list of steady income, then you can start to outsource some tasks to other freelancers or a virtual assistant. You can easily offload simple tasks to a VA or other freelancers. For example, if you are a writer, you can hire an editor to edit your work and save you some time having to self-edit.

When you start to hire other people, this is where freelancing can turn into an agency.

For example, if you are a social media manager, once you have built up a good base of clients, you can start hiring other freelancers, that you pay a little less while you act as the project manager or agency manager. So in that type of freelancing, you can generate passive income. However, at this point, it isn't really freelancing as much as building a different business.

There are other ways in which you can create passive income as a freelancer. For example, if you are a social media manager, you can set up accounts for your clients and then invest in some automation software to free up some of your time. If there is any way that you can set up automation systems for what you are currently doing, then you certainly can create passive income streams from your freelancing.

HOW AND WHY TO REINVEST YOUR EARNED INCOME

As with building any business, you should be reinvesting some of your earned income. Any good business owner knows this. But just sticking money back into your business willy nilly isn't going to get you anywhere. You need to know how, why, and what you should be reinvesting in.

I mentioned outsourcing certain tasks in the previous section, but I want to address it here a little differently. Outsourcing can be great for many reasons, mostly because it will give you more time to either do the leisure things you want to do or to work on other areas of your business. Outsourcing some of your tasks allows you to work ON your business rather than IN your business.

Outsourcing

There are also some disadvantages to outsourcing. First of all, it costs money, sometimes a lot, sometimes a little. If you have never managed anyone before, it can be quite an experience. Some people need very little direction to get their work done while others need to be micromanaged. You don't want to hire someone who needs micromanaging. Furthermore, if you outsource to someone who isn't very good, then you have to worry about letting them go and so on. One particular challenge of living the RV life and outsourcing your work is that it can be rather difficult to connect with your team, whether there are drastic differences in time zones or poor WiFi connection.

If you are planning to outsource to someone overseas to try and save some money, do your research! Platforms like onlinejobs.ph offer coaching services for your "employees" for a monthly cost. This is a great option if you have never built a team before and you don't know the first thing about how to manage someone. You can find virtual assistants on onlinejobs.ph in just about every specialty, from Amazon listing specialists to digital content creators. The great thing about hiring someone overseas is that their cost of living is lower. So if you are just starting out hiring a virtual assistant, this can be a great place to start without having to reinvest too much.

Automation

Another area to reinvest your earned income is into automation services. While it depends on your business model, there are a ton of different automation services out there that can help you to complete a variety of tasks.

Take social media management, for example. While you could spend about an hour or so a day scheduling things to Pinterest (per client!), that isn't the best use of your time. If you invested in a Pinterest scheduler - Tailwind is currently the most popular - then you can spend about an hour scheduling out one client's social media for the next month. You just saved yourself about 20-30 hours over the next month! Keep in mind that in this particular example, the client would pay the monthly subscription for Tailwind, not you. Plus, there are plenty of other kinds of automation software out there to help you to automate your business process.

As a freelancer, you can automate a number of your processes. With your email, for example, you can have emails automatically go into certain folders and check them in bulk at certain times rather than sifting through a bunch of unrelated emails. You can also set up processes to have clients automatically book calls with you rather than having to email back and forth to find a time to connect.

You can also automate part of your client onboarding process. This can be done with automated emails and project management tools. However, you want to be very careful with this part; you don't want to pull yourself out of the equation too much. While your client may have hired you to get them results, they are sure to still want to be in contact with you during your working relationship.

While automation is great for saving you time, there are also things that you can do to streamline your processes. For example, you can use a time tracking software that connects to your bookkeeping software to make sending invoices easier. This way you won't have to go through a huge spreadsheet of working times or guess how much time you spent on a project and how much you should invoice someone.

Professional development

You can also reinvest your earned income into continuing your education. This is a big one, freelancers that stay on top of their game are always working to improve themselves. There are so many online courses out there to help you advance your skills. If you are buying a course from an individual just make sure that you do your research, make sure they actually have experience doing what they say they do. You don't want to take a course on copywriting from someone who hasn't or doesn't actually make a living as a copywriter.

If you are unsure of where to start reinvesting your income when it comes to courses and education, Udemy is a great place to start. Udemy offers courses on just about any subject you can think of, from copywriting to Javascript. Their courses are led by reputable and expert instructors and are very affordable. They often run sales where you can get a course for as little as $12.

If you are looking for anything related to online marketing, such as content creation, copywriting, or SEO, then DigitalMarketer.com offers a huge array of both free and paid resources to expand your learning.

When you continually improve your skills, you can offer more value to your clients. When you offer more value, you can charge a lot more without having to work more. Take writing a sales copy letter, for example. When you can show clients results from previous experience and prove that your work will increase their ROI, you can increase your prices without having to worry about losing business.

Online presence

How you present yourself online can make or break your career as a freelancer. If you have a very ugly website (because you are a writer and not a web designer), then that can reflect poorly on you and the quality of work that you do. Now it is not to say that you won't get any work if you have an ugly website, but it can certainly negatively impact your business. Investing in having a strong online presence can help you to land better and higher-paying clients. This could mean investing in a web designer, a social media manager, or a coach to help you take your freelancing business to the next level.

Marketing

Marketing is something that you should never skimp on when it comes to building a business. In order to land clients, they have to know that you exist! Every business should have a marketing budget, whether it's large or small, some of your earned income should be going back into marketing to find new clients. This can be done with things like Facebook Ads, promoted pins to blog posts, or even for attending a conference.

The great thing about being able to invest your earned income back into your freelance business is that living the RV lifestyle allows you less monthly, personal bills that you have to worry about paying. This can leave you with a good chunk of change at the end of each month to reinvest back into your business, which means that you can also grow it quicker.

CHAPTER SUMMARY

Freelancing is a great way to get started making an income online. You can take skills that you already have and turn them into a freelance career. You can either be hired by a company to freelance or work with clients individually; it is ultimately up to you based on your goals.

You can find freelance work through freelance platforms and job boards.

While there is not much passive income when you start out freelancing, there are certain things you can do to work less and make more, such as via outsourcing and automating to increase your passive income.

In order to continue to grow your business, there are certain areas that you should reinvest your earned income back into, such as hiring someone to outsource work to and investing in automation systems and personal development.

CHAPTER RESOURCES

Healthcare for independent freelancers

- HealthCare.Gov

Types of freelance work

- Voiceover artist
- Writer/copywriter/ghostwriter/blogger
- Web design
- Graphic design
- Virtual assistant
- Social media manager
- Translation
- Transcription
- Illustration
- Data Entry
- SEO specialist
- Video editor
- Songwriter
- Game development
- Mobile app development
- Ecommerce
- Consulting

- Greeting card designer

Outsourcing

- Onlinejobs.ph

Professional development

- Udemy
- DigitalMarketer.com

Freelance platforms

- Facebook
- UpWork
- Fiverr
- Freelancer
- Envato Studio
- PeoplePerHour-Great for those located in the UK
- TopTal-Great if you are already an expert in your field

Job boards for freelancers

- Problogger
- ZipRecruiter
- Indeed

- Glassdoor
- LinkedIn
- SmashingJobs-great for developers
- BloggingPro
- MediaBistro
- SoloGig
- JournalismJobs
- WeWorkRemotly
- Online Writing Jobs
- Freelance Writing
- All Freelance Writing

In the next chapter, we will cover exactly how you can make passive income by self-publishing books.

CHAPTER THREE
Mastering The Art Of
Self-Publishing For Profit

Have you ever dreamed of being a writer? Sitting on the beach with your toes in the sand while you pen your newest manuscript?

The days of having to go through publishing houses and dealing with publishing agents is over. Once your manuscript is complete, you can self-publish it on online platforms and start making money in as little as 24 hours.

In this chapter, we are going to cover what exactly self-publishing is, how you can select a profitable niche, how and where to publish your first eBook, whether you should write the book yourself or outsource it, why you need a cover that grabs your potential reader by the eyeballs, when you should definitely turn your ebook into an audiobook (and when you shouldn't), and finally, whether you should stick to one publishing platform or spread your book out everywhere.

WHAT EXACTLY IS SELF-PUBLISHING?

Self-publishing is just that, a book that you publish yourself.

You write the book then publish it on free platforms like Amazon without ever having it have to be accepted by a publisher or waiting years for a royalty check. The great thing about self-publishing is that you have full control over your book and you get to keep a lot more of the royalties from sales rather than having to share with a publishing house.

When you publish a book through a publishing house there are many restrictions that are placed on the publication. For example, if you wanted to give away a chapter of your book to help get people interested, you can't do that if you are working with a publisher unless they approve. If you are self-publishing your book you can give away a chapter, or heck, even a few free copies to get the word out and have people leave you reviews.

So now that you know what self-publishing actually is, how do you go about knowing what you should write about that people will actually want to pay for to read?

SELECTING A NICHE THAT WILL MAKE YOU MONEY

It's likely that you have a ton of different ideas for book topics. But you don't just want to write about any old topic. You want to write about something that is going to sell and that people actually want to read!

If you haven't already written your book, you are going to want to validate your idea first, before you ever even write your first word. You can do this simply by searching your competition on Amazon.

Search the various categories on Amazon for Kindle best sellers in the eBook category. Within that category you will find many sub-categories such as happiness, motivational, and personal development. Pick a topic that you want to write about or have started writing about and check out what the top sellers are.

When it comes to sizing up the competition, you want to take a look at that book's Amazon Best Sellers Ranking. You want all the books on the first page of results to have an average BSR of 100,000 or less. Anything above 100,000 shows that the demand for that subject isn't optimal and there are fewer people buying books on that subject.

The second thing you want to look at is how many reviews the books on the first page have, if it's all big authoritative names with hundreds or thousands of reviews you might not be able to compete. However, this is not a hard and fast rule, you have to consider the niche you are writing about. While it might be difficult to get to the #1 best seller for personal development and beat out some very high profile authors, you can certainly size up and beat the competition in a niche like opening a dog boarding business.

The best seller ranking is assigned to a book based on how much it sells. It really all comes down to keywords. The more targeted the book is to an audience, the more likely that the audience is going to purchase that book to solve their problem, and, therefore, the more your book is going to sell.

There are a few other things that you should consider when writing your book. Make sure that you are writing about something that you're passionate about. You don't want to spend months or weeks writing about something you have no interest in. You should also make sure that you are knowledgeable about the topic (it's ok if you aren't, we'll get to that in a minute). It is great if you are writing a book to share your knowledge with the world, but in reality, if you want to write a book on a topic that you don't know much about but you think will sell well, you can always outsource the actual writing.

Now that you have a firm grasp on what your book is going to be about, or perhaps you already have written it, it's time to move onto publishing!

HOW TO PUBLISH YOUR VERY FIRST BOOK-WHAT YOU NEED TO INCLUDE

The hard part is over, you have written your book and are ready to publish it. Self-publishing a book isn't nearly as scary as it sounds. If you are starting on Amazon, which is suggested, the process of uploading your book is very simple.

You want to be sure that your topic is something that people want to read about. Remember, a little bit of competition is a good thing, that means people are buying similar products. Your title and subtitle should grab the reader's attention and address their pain points. When someone reads your title they should want to click the buy now button right away!

An attention grabbing cover

You should also ensure that your book has a cover that is going to grab your reader's attention. The cover should have a clear message and not be too cluttered as to confuse people. Cover design is something that many people outsource, because unless you are already a graphic designer, you aren't going to get the best quality by doing it yourself.

Formatting

You also need to ensure that your book looks great on the inside. Formatting is key here. You don't want huge blocks of text that aren't broken up. Instead, break text into sections, use Bulleted or numbered lists, and images to make the inside of the book more visually appealing. The book should be easy to read as well as easy to scan. Amazon actually offers a mock up type generator that allows you to see what the inside of your look will look like once it has been published on their platform.

Book description

The description of your book is also very important. It is really less of a description and more of a sales letter (Awosika, 2019). This is where you need to focus on your audiences' pain points and how they will be solved when they read your book. The description should really focus on the benefits that the book will provide to the reader.

Using freelancers

Fiverr and Upwork are great platforms to hire freelancers to help you with your book. You can hire freelancers to help you write or ghostwrite the actual book, and book cover designers to help you with developing and creating the most eye-catching cover for your book's niche. You can also hire freelance editors, formatters, and even marketers. Hiring a freelancer is a wonderful option, not only are you helping other entrepreneurs build their business, but you can also find some amazing freelancers for affordable prices.

SHOULD YOU WRITE YOUR BOOK YOURSELF OR OUTSOURCE IT?

There is a dirty little secret in the world of online self-publishing, not all authors write their own books!

I'm just letting all the secrets out!

That's ok though. You see, books can take a very long time to write and if you are a business owner that is running another business, or several other businesses, you might not have time to sit down and write a book. Or perhaps you really want to write a book about a specific topic, such as finances or a fiction romance novel, but you don't have enough knowledge to write an entire book. Or maybe, you just aren't a very good writer.

This is where outsourcing your work will come in handy.

There are plenty of great writers out there that freelance their writing services. They do all the heavy lifting of writing the book, in collaboration with the author of course, then publish it under the author's name. This is called ghostwriting.

There are just as many authors out there who write their own books. If you love writing and you have a strong message or story that you want to tell your audience, then you can probably handle writing your own book.

CREATING A STUNNING AND EYE-CATCHING COVER

People really do judge a book by its cover. While it is good to have some ideas in mind about what you want your cover to look like, you should not even worry about cover design until you have a solid title and subtitle down.

You are going to want to be sure that the cover of your book is sending a clear message and sticking to the norms of the genre's style. Check out the other books in the same genre and take note of what their covers look like. Find your inspiration from other Amazon Kindle best sellers. Perhaps there are certain colors that really stick out to you and catch your eye or types of font you find appealing.

You can also look to social media, specifically Pinterest, for book cover inspiration. Search by genre, topic, color, and niche to find different ideas. Why not try making your own Pinterest board and save all of your great inspiration for when it comes time to design the cover?

While some book covers can be easy to design if you have some skills, you might need to outsource if you are looking for something a little more complicated. If you are looking to design the cover yourself, there are plenty of free templates and tutorials available online. Some great resources for designing the book cover yourself are Canva, Microsoft Word, or Adobe Photoshop and InDesign. If you don't have much experience in design, Canva is a great, user-friendly software to start with.

If you want to leave the cover design to a design professional, there are also many platforms that offer eBook cover design services. Reedsy is a great platform where you can get not only an eBook cover, but also interior design as well by industry leading designers for an affordable price. EBook Launch is another great platform in which you can get eBook covers of all kinds, for fiction, illustrated, and non-fiction.

When you are designing your cover or having a designer do it for you, just make sure you are getting the dimensions of the cover correct. Generally speaking for an Amazon cover it is 2,560 x 1,600 pixels; however, it can change depending on which publication platform you are using. So ensure that you double check the size ratio before designing or having your cover designed.

SHOULD YOU TURN YOUR BOOK INTO AN AUDIOBOOK?

The use of audiobooks has grown exponentially over the past couple of years. While people love to sit down with a good book, they don't always have the time. Purchasing an audiobook allows them to consume the book faster and while they are doing other activities, such as chores, commuting, or working out.

On average, individuals who listen to audiobooks listen to about 15 a year. While the barrier to entry is fairly low for a written book to self-publish on just about any platform, there is a little more involved if you are looking to publish an audiobook as well.

ACX.com is the number one platform when it comes to publishing your audiobook. ACX is a part of Audible and helps to bring together creators, narrators, recording engineers, and even publishers to make you more money with your audiobook. With ACX, your audiobook can be published on Audible, Amazon.com, and iTunes in order to maximize your profits across all platforms. You can audition narrators to find the perfect voice for your book. ACX makes the whole process seamless from making your account to collecting your royalties.

The biggest thing with audiobooks is that you need really high quality sound. While it takes more time and effort to publish an audiobook, in addition to the eBook, the potential profits can be huge, considering the continued growth of the audiobook market.

Now you might think that creating an audiobook isn't for your audience, or that YOU could never narrate your book. First of all, everyone listens to audiobooks!

From the CEO on his/her commute to the office to the stay at home mom driving her kids to band practice, many people from many walks of life listen to audiobooks. The simple fact is if you don't create an audiobook as a companion to your written eBook, you are leaving money on the table that could be going into your pocket (Chesson, 2019a)!

A word of caution though, there are simply some books that do not make good audiobooks. Things like reference or quote books, anything that is very image heavy, such as interior design books, cookbooks, and travel guides. So if your book is one of these, then don't worry about creating an audiobook, it is not going to serve your audience. However, if you are writing romance, health and fitness, business, self-help, history, mystery, or anything related to any of these topics (Chesson, 2019a), then an audiobook is a fantastic idea!

Audiobooks come in many different formats and files, so be sure you are really looking into what type of file is needed before you dive into the creation process. Generally, audiobooks are MP3, M4B, or WAV files. You are also going to have to create another cover for your audiobook, 2400 by 2400 pixels. If you have no idea what that means, don't worry, you can get a cover made on Fiverr for $5.

While recording the audiobook yourself is a very economical option, you can also hire a voice over artist and sound engineer to do the mastering for you.

If you are choosing to record your own audiobook you must ensure that you have quality equipment, which can be an investment in itself if you don't already have it. Things like microphones, headphones, audio interfacing devices, sound eliminators, acoustic equipment, and adequate file storage, and recording/editing software can all add up to hundreds of dollars. If you are planning on doing the narration yourself for multiple books, it might be a worthwhile investment.

However, if you are just starting out and don't want to worry about purchasing a bunch of new equipment, then hiring a voice over artist would be beneficial. The cost of hiring a voice over artist can vary widely depending on many factors; however, it is wise to budget $50 to $200 per finished hour of narration. The price can vary greatly depending on the experience and the quality of the narration. With the ACX.com platform you can find high quality narration talent for $50, which is very affordable and well worth the cost.

Even if you do record everything yourself, send off your recording to an audio engineer. For a rather small cost this can really give your audiobook the pizzaz that it needs upon completion. Also ensure that you are creating a cover specifically for your audiobook. It can be the same design, but adjust the design to match the dimensions for the audiobook distributor.

I have talked a lot about eBooks and audiobooks, but there is one format of book that we haven't covered yet. The paperback or hardcover book. While many people prefer eBooks and listening to audio-books, you can never discount the classic paperback and hardcover. The smell of a freshly printed book, that crack of the spine the first time you open it, there is nothing else like it. I'm sure I am not the only person to feel this way, so why not cater to your physical book lovers as well?

The great thing about already having an eBook is that you can easily have a physical book printed. And no, I am not talking about ordering 10,000 copies and paying for them in advance just to have them sit in a storage unit somewhere. KDP has the ability to print physical books on demand. One of the best things about print on demand paperback and hardcover books is that you don't have to worry about having a bunch of copies printed right away, but rather you can have them printed as the customer orders them. This can save you a ton of money and frustration.

HOW AND WHY YOU SHOULD DISTRIBUTE YOUR BOOK ON MULTIPLE PLATFORMS

When it comes to the distribution of your book, you have several options. You can choose to publish on Kindle Unlimited or Kindle Select, but this then prohibits you from publishing your book on any other platforms. Or you can publish it as a regular Kindle book and then publish to other platforms like Kobo, Barnes & Noble, or iTunes.

There are several benefits to enrolling into Kindle Unlimited.

- You can put your book on sale for a limited time to create urgency to drive sales.
- You can offer your book for free for a limited time.
- As opposed to getting paid per book you get a cut of the Kindle Unlimited "pool."
- Being part of the Kindle Unlimited and Kindle Owners Lending Library can help to increase your Amazon search rankings (Chesson, 2017).

There are also advantages to publishing your eBook on multiple platforms as well. While Amazon has a GIANT reach, it can also be good to spread things out on different platforms as well. Even if you do only get a small percentage of your sales from other publishing platforms that aren't Amazon, that small percentage can really add up over time.

With Kindle, there are audiences that just don't use the Kindle platform to consume their books and can't use it for one reason or another. Having your book available on other platforms allows for a wider audience in some cases. A platform like Kobo actually has an in-house marketing team to help you get everything up and running.

Using ads to drive traffic to your book

With either Amazon or various other platforms, you can also consider using ads to drive sales to your books rather than just marketing on the platform itself. The biggest thing you have to remember is that no matter which platform you choose, your sales are not guaranteed. You have to be able to actively market your book to your audience in order to get sales. You can't just hit publish and cross your fingers, that is not going to get you very many sales.

While learning about running ads for selling your product (in this case your book) can be a little overwhelming when you are first starting out, there are a few basics to consider. There are two kinds of ads that you can run: automatic and manual. If you are serious about running ads you might want to look into hiring someone to do so as you can quickly lose a lot of money on ads if you don't know what you are doing.

Automatic ads are just that, plug and play - put in a budget, and let your ads run. This can be a great first option if you aren't very familiar with running ads. Just make sure not to set your budget too high. Manual ads require bidding on keywords and keeping a close eye on how your ads are performing. Once you get the hang of it, manual ads aren't as scary as they sound and can greatly help you to drive sales to your book. Running ads are all about keywords - you need to know the keywords you are targeting to generate any kind of traction with your ads.

The platform you choose to publish your book on can vary widely by your audience as well too. It will likely take some time and some experimentation before you figure out what works for you and what resonates with your audience. There are no rules against writing several books and publishing them on various platforms to see what works better for you and your audience. Test, test, and test some more to find out what works, then do more of what works.

Here is a list just to get you started on various platforms that you can publish your book on:

- Amazon Kindle
- Kobo
- Barnes and Noble
- iBook/iTunes
- CreateSpace
- LuLu
- Blurb
- BookBaby
- Bookrix
- Scribd
- Outskirts Press

Just to name a few...

While it can be a lot of work to self-publish a book, especially if you are going to spread your book out through various different platforms, there are tools to make it a lot easier. Platforms like Draft2Digital, Smashwords, and PublishDrive assist in the distribution of your book, help to collect and analyze the book's analytics, collect royalties for you, and pay you out in one transaction rather than having to collect from multiple platforms.

Once your book really starts to take off and you are getting loads of PR, then you can travel to each of your book signings while living your RV life! Not sure how to get PR? You can hire someone for that too!

CHAPTER SUMMARY

You can easily publish a book and start making money is as little as 24 hours. When you self-publish you have full control over the creative process and distribution of your book.

Certain niches are much more profitable than others. Search the Amazon Kindle best sellers list to see what kinds of topics get purchased the most. Shoot for topics that are somewhere between 1,000 and 30,000 on the Kindle best sellers list. But also make sure that you are choosing a topic that you are passionate about.

You can be an author without having to be a great writer. There are many writers that outsource the writing process. Once the book is written it is time to hit publish! Amazon makes it very easy to publish your book with only a few clicks.

Make people want to buy your book with an eye catching cover design, a great title, and attention grabbing sub-title. Put your book into Amazon's mockup generator to ensure that the inside of your book is just as appealing. Your book description should be able to speak to your audience's pain points and address how reading your book can help them.

You can become a self-published author even if you aren't great at writing and don't have the time to write a book. You can outsource the writing to a ghostwriter and still retain the rights to everything.

Take inspiration for your book cover from other book covers in the same genre. You can either design a cover yourself or you can outsource this as well.

Audiobooks are becoming more popular but are more work to get published. Audiobooks are easier to consume and you can generate more profit from them. You can record the audiobook if you already have high quality sound equipment, or you can outsource to a voice over artist.

There are benefits and downfalls to publishing your book on Amazon or on multiple platforms. Ultimately, you need to decide what is best for you and your audience. You can also increase sales by running ads to your book. You need to be sure that you are actively marketing your book, not just hitting publish and waiting for a check to roll in.

If you want to focus on PR, you can hire someone to handle that for you also.

CHAPTER RESOURCES

eBook Cover design

- Canva
- Adobe Photoshop and InDesign
- Reedsy
- EBook Launch
- Fiverr
- Upwork

eBook/audiobook Distribution

- Draft2Digital
- Smashwords
- PublishDrive

Self-Publishing Platforms

- Amazon Kindle
- Kobo
- Barnes and Noble
- iBook/iTunes

- CreateSpace
- LuLu
- Blurb
- BookBaby
- Bookrix
- Scribd
- Outskirts Press
- ACX.com

The next chapter is all about how to earn a great income as a blogger.

CHAPTER FOUR
How To Build A Blogging Business For Sustainable Income

Blogging, just like many other businesses, is what you make of it. The time and effort you put into it, especially in the beginning, will determine how successful you are and ultimately how much money you can make from it. There are well-known bloggers that are making six-figures per month while traveling full time in their RVs.

In this chapter, we are going to cover what exactly blogging is, what the differences are between a journaling site, an authority site, and a niche site. I will also discuss exactly how bloggers make money and how you can apply those concepts to make money with your own blog and how to get people to actually read your blog. Finally, I'll also review what SEO is and why it's so important to your blog.

WHAT IS BLOGGING - IN A NUTSHELL

Way back when the internet was just a baby, people would start online journals, otherwise known as weblogs. As Skrba explains, "A blog (shortening of "weblog") is an online journal or informational website displaying information in reverse chronological order, with the latest posts appearing first. It is a platform where a writer or even a group of writers share their views on an individual subject."

There are many, many websites that either started as a blog or have a blog that is used to promote content to help drive leads to their business. There are two main reasons why someone starts a blog, either for personal reasons or to increase their business' visibility. As a business, if you also have a blog this provides you with more opportunities to gain customers and stay competitive.

JOURNALING VS. AUTHORITY VS. NICHE SITES, WHAT'S THE BEST?

While there are two main reasons to start a blog, there are three distinct types of blogs - journaling, authority, and niche blogs.

Journaling blogs are often started as a personal blog and either stay that way or end up developing into a business driven blog. This can happen after the blogger realizes that their online journaling has struck a chord with a certain audience, and they can actually make money while doing what they love.

Then there are authority sites, such as BuzzFeed, Huffington Post, and The Wirecutter. They can focus on one type of content, in the case of a site like Forbes, or they can focus on a variety of content. The truth is when it comes to authority sites, there isn't much to compete with.

Niche sites, on the other hand, focus on a very specific niche or topic. For example, rather than a site/blog that has only a few popular articles on the RV lifestyle, a niche site would be dedicated to that specific topic. Everything they promote and write about would focus on living the RV lifestyle.

HOW BLOGGERS MAKE MONEY AND HOW YOU CAN TO!

It seems like every day there are more ways that bloggers can earn a great income. As I stated before, there are bloggers out there that are making six-figures per month! While this might not be the most common outcome for many bloggers, there are still a vast number who make a really good income that allows them the freedom to travel full time, whether in an RV or not. There are a few main ways that bloggers can earn money:

- Ads
- Sponsorships
- Digital products
- Affiliate sales
- Services

When you start a self-hosted blog you have the ability to place ads on your site. Self-hosting a blog just means that you are paying a company to host your blog and all of its information. This also means that your domain is something like: mygreatsite.com rather than mygreatsite.wordpress.com. This not only looks much more professional, it's easier to say, and you have WAY more control over what you do with your blog.

By far, Wordpress is the best platform for blogging. It is incredibly easy to use and over a quarter of the internet is run on Wordpress sites. There are two different types of Wordpress sites: Wordpress.com and Wordpress.org. Wordpress.com sites have a domain with something like mygreatsite.wordpress.com, whereas with Wordpress.org you purchase a domain and install Wordpress on your site. So your domain would be something like mygreatsite.com.

I talked a little bit about this earlier but it is worth mentioning again.

There are lots of different blogging platforms but using Wordpress is going to give you the most flexibility with your site. Wordpress users have access to thousands of different plugins to allow you to do just about anything you could ever want to do to and with your site, from adding a storefront to creating quizzes. Wordpress is trusted by some of the biggest bloggers out there and also offers great customer service if you ever run into any issues.

Ads

Ad companies pay you, the blogger, to have ads on your site. There are many different ad networks available. One of the most popular for bloggers that are just starting out is Google Adsense. While they don't pay a whole lot, it is a way to get your foot in the door. The great thing about ad income is that it is passive. Once you have the ads set up on your blog, you will continue to get a payout as long as you are getting enough traffic to your blog.

Sponsorships

The next type of income is sponsorships. This is a great way to generate a good and consistent income for your blog. While it can take a little time to start getting opportunities, once you have a few that you can work with on a consistent basis, you can generate a reliable income. Sponsorships can either be one off sponsored posts or a continued working relationship with another company to promote their products and or services to your audience. This can take place through writing blog posts, posting about the company on your social media, sending out information in your email newsletter, or even making a short video.

Digital products

Digital products are another great way to create a passive income stream for your blog. Once you create them you can keep making money from them without much upkeep. Digital products can be anything from ebooks, courses, guides, print-ables, just about anything that you can create in a digital format that your audience will buy and you don't have to continually work on. You can sell your digital products directly through your blog or use a digital product platform, such as Shopify, Etsy or Clickbank. You can also choose to do both and market your digital products on various platforms. Generally speaking, the more places you are in, the more income you can generate.

Affiliate sales

Affiliate sales can also be another great way to generate some passive income. Here is a great example of how you can create multiple passive income streams from affiliate sales. Say you write a blog post promoting a particular product which pays a pretty good commission, either a one time or recurring commission. You build up a good audience or by chance your post goes viral. Many people are reading your post and decide to purchase the product based on your review or recommendation. You only wrote the post once but you keep earning a commission from it. While you might have to work on marketing the post here and there, it is mostly passive income.

You can also build entire businesses that are based on affiliate commissions. More on this in Chapter Six.

Services

Lastly, there are services. This is the least passive income model for blogging. Services require you to either work one-on-one with clients or with a group of clients. This can be things like running membership sites, conferences, mastermind calls, personal coaching, or other freelance type services, like design or social media management. Services can be a great way to earn a lot of income but they are more time consuming.

Using blogging to create multiple streams of income

The great thing about blogging is that you don't have to choose just one of these ways to earn money from your blog, you can choose to use all of them or just a few of these strategies. While it is pretty simple to start out using ads and affiliate income for blogging, adding digital products, sponsorships, and services takes a little more time to get things going. However, you can work on creating various income streams from your blog by incorporating different ways to earn income.

However, in order to earn any kind of income from your blog you need to get people to visit it first and become fans. You need to be able to find a large audience of readers who are willing to buy things from you, whether as an affiliate or things that you personally create.

WHERE YOU FIND YOUR AUDIENCE AND GET EYEBALLS ON YOUR SITE

When you first start a blog, actually getting traffic to your site and people to read your content can seem rather overwhelming with all the other blogs and websites already taking up their attention. If you don't understand how to market and how to use SEO to your advantage (we'll get to this in the next section), then it will be difficult for people to find you online.

Just as with many things in blogging, there are literally tons of different ways to get people to read your blog. The trick is to get them to read it and then buy something from you. Besides, the key here is to actually make a living from blogging.

There are many different ways to drive traffic to your site.

Just to name a few...

- Facebook posts
- Facebook ads
- Instagram posts
- Instagram ads

- Twitter posts
- SEO
- Pinterest pins
- Pinterest ads
- YouTube videos
- Adwords campaigns
- Backlinking

You see how this can get pretty confusing pretty quick?

Getting people to visit your site also depends on where your audience hangs out online. For example, if you are starting a food blog, Pinterest is a great place to start driving people to your website. If you are creating a blog on something that is already popular on a certain platform, use that platform to drive traffic to your blog.

Using social media to drive traffic

There are a few reasons why it's a great idea to use social media to start driving traffic to your blog. First of all, you don't have to buy ads, it's free (except for maybe paying automation software). Yes, you heard me right, it doesn't cost you anything to set up business accounts on Pinterest, Facebook, Twitter, Instagram or any other social network. You can post, as a blog/business, rather than using a personal account, and start getting traffic to your site.

SEO *for traffic*

Growing your blog using social media is great if you blog about topics that your friends and family would talk about or share on the various social media platforms (Marrow, 2019). These are topics like weight loss, health, parenting, DIY activities, or food. Using SEO is great for topics that people search for online. This can include product reviews (think "the best…"), how-to type information, or things you would ask an expert, like: "What is the best Wordpress plugin for creating a Table of Contents?"

Most likely, unless your friends and family are also bloggers, you are not going to be sitting around the table discussing Wordpress themes and plugins. This is where SEO is really going to give you a leg up. A good rule of thumb is to keep the posts on your site about 50/50. That is 50 percent on content that is highly shareable (list posts, how-tos, etc) while the other half should be searchable content (the best…).

Utilizing SEO is a great, and free, way to generate traffic to your site.

WHAT IS SEO AND WHY IT'S SO IMPORTANT

When you are just getting started with blogging the term SEO can be very intimidating. It can seem like this big magical thing that only the big dogs have a full understanding of. I can promise you, SEO is not as scary or difficult as you think. It is actually quite a simple process that anyone can learn in order to help bring traffic to their blog.

Moz, a very well known company that provides a high quality SEO tool, defines SEO as: "SEO stands for Search Engine Optimization. It's the practice of increasing both the quality and quantity of website traffic, as well as exposure to your brand, through non-paid (also known as 'organic') search engine results."

It is all about keywords. Many years ago, you could write a post and just keyword stuff, meaning that whatever keyword(s) you were trying to rank for you could just write it in the post a bunch of times. However, this didn't always make for great reading. This is when the search engines got smart. Search engines can now determine if you are writing a post simply to get ranked or to actually help your readers. If you are writing a post just to get it ranked, most likely you are not going to end up on the first page of Google. If you are writing your content with the intention of actually helping people, then there is a good chance that your articles will get ranked pretty high on Google's search results, which makes it easier for people to find you.

It also doesn't cost you anything to rank in Google, other than a lot of time and effort. You need to continually provide your audience with valuable and useful content that benefits your audience rather than just writing to get noticed by the search engines.

When you are writing your blog and focusing on search engine optimization, you need to understand user intent. There are three different kinds of user intent, those that are searching for information, those that are searching for a specific website, and those that are searching to purchase something.

In addition to understanding what the user intent for your audience is, you must also understand what your blog's goals are. Is your goal just to get people to sign up for your newsletter so you can market to them again later on, or are you looking to get them to buy something from you right away?

SEO really isn't a stand alone thing that you should be working towards on your blog, it is a means to a much bigger end. While using strategic SEO tactics can certainly help you to rank high on Google and other search engine results pages, just ranking on a search engine isn't going to help you unless people are clicking through to your site. In addition, it doesn't matter how many people are clicking through to your site but how many people are contributing to your larger business goals, such as buying something through an affiliate link.

While it is pretty awesome to see your site listed on the first page of Google, the bottom line, if it is not helping you to make money or achieve some other business goal, it's not doing you much good. The great thing about SEO is that you can continually work towards improving it on your site. It is fairly easy to see what your competitors are doing with their SEO strategies and to be able to learn from them in order to improve your SEO strategy.

If you are trying to get your blog ranked high in Google for something, search that term in Google and see what kinds of keywords are coming up in the autosuggest. When you figure out which of your competitors are ranking high for that specific keyword, then take a look at their site. How is the article structured? How are they using variations of the keyword(s) to get higher in the search rankings while still providing value to the audience? And most importantly, how can you do it better?

If the thought of SEO and all things related to search engines still scare you, don't worry, this is another area of your business that you can easily outsource.

CHAPTER SUMMARY

In its simplest form, a blog is an informational website made up of posts. All blogs are websites, but not all websites are blogs. Blogs are used by companies to help drive sales to their products and services.

Journaling blogs start out as personal blogs and then often develop into a business. Authority sites are very large, often cover a wider range of topics, and have teams of writers, editors, and people to manage the site. Niche blogs, while they can be large, focus on a more narrow topic.

Bloggers earn money in the following ways:

- Ads
- Sponsorships
- Digital products
- Affiliate sales
- Services

When blogging for business, you should always have a self-hosted site. This gives you more control over your site and how you can make money with it.

You can focus on one of the aforementioned revenue streams or you can use all of them to generate multiple streams of income from your blog.

There are many ways to get traffic to your blog:

- Facebook posts
- Facebook ads
- Instagram posts
- Instagram ads
- Twitter posts
- SEO
- Pinterest pins
- Pinterest ads
- YouTube videos
- Adwords campaigns
- Backlinking

You can drive traffic to your blog either through using social media or implementing SEO (Search Engine Optimization) tactics. The main thing to remember when you are working on a post and trying to optimize it for the search engines and your reader is user intent.

SEO is a means to a much larger end. You have to consider your blog's goals other than just trying to get on the first page of Google.

While it is good to have a solid understanding of SEO, you can also outsource to help drive more organic traffic to your blog.

CHAPTER RESOURCES

Where to sell digital products

- Shopify
- Etsy
- Clickbank

In the next chapter, I will reveal the secrets of making money on YouTube.

CHAPTER FIVE
YouTube Success
Secrets Revealed

Y OUTUBE HAS QUICKLY become a platform for entrepreneurs to make a great living. Just as with other digital nomad type business models available to those wanting to live the RV life, YouTube is a great option that offers flexibility while being able to build a fairly passive income business. People love watching videos and it is a landscape that is not going to change in the near future. While creating a YouTube channel on its own is great, it is also a great compliment for any kind of content creator - bloggers, freelancers, comedians, artists, and so on.

In this chapter, we are going to review how to get started on YouTube, an overview of creating your first video, how to grow your subscriber base so that you can monetize your channel, why you should document your RV adventures for your subscribers, how you can get paid actively and passively using this platform, and how you can use YouTube ads to generate a great passive income.

HOW TO GET STARTED WITH YOUTUBE

Getting started with YouTube is very easy, but just like with any other business you are both a creator and a business owner. As you are running a YouTube business you need to think of it *as a business* and have clear goals in mind. Really think about your goals before you jump into creating your channel. Do you just want to document your RV journey (also referred to as vlogging)? If so, what is going to make your channel unique and make people want to watch your videos?

Now, it's not to say that you need a channel that is totally unique, there are plenty of channels out there that document people traveling in their RV, but what about you or your channel is going to be able to give you an edge?

Take a look at other similar, popular channels that cover the same kinds of topics that you want to cover. What kinds of things do they cover in their videos? How are they branding themselves and their channels? What about the production of their videos?

How can you come up with a channel that shows the true you (don't be fake!) and offers something different to your audience?

When starting your channel you don't need anything more than a good quality phone camera (which you probably already have) and a computer. You don't need to worry about fancy and expensive cameras to start with. Many successful YouTubers have started with just the bare minimum and worked their way up to bigger and better equipment once they actually started to make money.

Creating your YouTube channel takes a lot of practice to get started, especially if you are not used to being on camera. You have to be willing to mess up and let go of your control if you are going to grow, learn and improve. You are not going to become a master at YouTube overnight, it is going to take hours and hours of refining your video skills. You don't have to be perfect to start getting subscribers and to grow your channel.

The biggest thing that you are going to need to make your videos look good is great lighting. You can either do this with natural lighting, which shouldn't be too much of an issue if you are traveling around in your RV, or use a simple light from the store that has the ability to have multiple bulbs turned on at once. Just make sure that whatever equipment that you do have will be able to easily fit into your RV and will travel well.

Creating content

In the process of getting everything started, it is good to brainstorm a ton of different video ideas, at minimum 50-100 different ideas. With YouTube you need to be able to put out content on a consistent basis, whether it is a 5-minute video per day or one 30 minute video per week, you need to be prepared to create enough content. Out of all the different ideas that you come up with, start with the first 10 or so that you are really excited about and that you think will do well based on your previous research. You also need to figure out what your filming and upload schedule is going to be. It's better to focus on quality over quantity but also to be able to be consistent with your schedule (Perkins, 2108).

The actual creation of your YouTube channel is super simple, especially if you already have a Gmail account as they are linked. You are going to want to make sure that you have a banner for your channel and that you write a good description that is SEO friendly. This simply means write a description that really defines what your channel is actually about using words that your audience would search for. A channel banner and a good description help to make your channel look more professional and can encourage people to subscribe to your channel.

Creating your first video

Now onto the fun part, the actual video creation! Unless you already have experience in public speaking or have been an actor or actress, your first couple of videos are going to be a little awkward. It's OK! Go look at some of the first videos of your favorite YouTubers, I can bet you that they aren't very good. It is better to create the content and get it out there rather than to try and be a perfectionist about everything.

After you have done all the fun filming, it is time to edit the video and design your thumbnail. Again, people judge things by their cover. You need to create an eye-catching thumbnail that is going to get your audience's attention and make them want to click on the video. When it comes to editing your videos, choose an editing software that is easy to use. If you are not already familiar with how to edit videos this can be just another thing that can cause you to feel overwhelmed. There are many simple editing software out there. If you own a Mac you should already have iMovie installed, if you own a PC, there is Windows Movie Creator, which are both very user-friendly. For a very user-friendly and affordable video editor, Filmora is also a great option.

After you have edited and uploaded your first video (and every subsequent video after) it is beneficial to give your video a little boost. While this might sound a little funny, you should like your own video, give it a comment saying something like leave a comment below, and share your video wherever possible. This can include your Facebook page, your Instagram, your Twitter, and your Pinterest accounts. Don't be afraid to ask your friends and family to watch your video and like, and or, leave a comment. Every little bit of exposure that you can get in the beginning is going to help! By nature, the more views a video has the more people are going to watch it due to social proof.

The biggest thing is consistency! You need to be consistent in making your videos and uploading them. It is much easier to grow your channel if you are uploading videos on a regular basis rather than only uploading them once and awhile. While it can take anywhere from six to twelve months to actually start seeing a good amount of growth, having consistency and producing quality videos with eye-catching thumbnails is definitely going to help you.

GROWING YOUR SUBSCRIBER BASE

In order to actually make money from YouTube you need to have people watch your videos and subscribe to your channel. First of all, when you are making videos, ASK your audience to subscribe to your channel and to hit the like button.

Create awesome content

Just as with other online businesses you can turn to social media or use SEO tactics to drive traffic to your videos. There are a few components to building your subscriber base on your YouTube channel. You first must be able to create awesome content that is unique, valuable, interesting, and high quality.

Collaborate with influencers

The second part of being able to grow your audience very quickly is to get in front of other people's audiences. In the blogging world, this can be done through guest posting. In YouTube, it can mean collaborating with other YouTubers or social media influencers in a variety of ways. This can be done through being featured on another YouTuber's video(s), being a guest on someone else's podcast, shout-outs on social media, and guest posting on their blog.

When you are reaching out to influencers to ask them to feature you, don't go after the big dogs. If you are just starting out it is likely that you will quickly get shut down. Go after influencers and other YouTubers that have a couple hundred or a couple thousand more followers than you do.

Remember, it's all about giving before you ask though. See what you can do for the blogger or YouTuber before you straight out ask them for something. People don't like that kind of stuff. As your audience grows, you can go after collaborating with influencers with bigger audiences. Keep in mind though, as you grow, reciprocate what others have done for you. Once your audience gets bigger and if someone asks you to collaborate, just remember what other influencers have done to help you out.

Quality over quantity

Before you even start reaching out to influencers you want to be sure that you are already creating stellar content. While there will always be vain people out there who only care about your follower count or number of views you have, more than likely they are going to care more about the type and quality of content you are putting out. Be sure that you are already providing your audience with a ton of value and are genuinely wanting to help people rather than just looking to inflate your numbers.

Now that you are ready to reach out to people and collaborate with them, it's time to start making a list. You are going to want to focus on people, again, that are just a few steps ahead of you, not miles. When you are reaching out to potential collaborators, make sure you actually have a pitch for them, rather than just asking them to help you without any sort of plan that also benefits them and their respective audiences.

Use other platforms to grow your subscribers

You can also look to social media to grow your subscriber base. If you already have an audience on platforms such as Pinterest, Facebook, Twitter, or Instagram, you can share your YouTube videos on your other profiles. Also make sure that you actually ask people to subscribe and like your videos when they are watching them on other channels as well.

Building your audience is going to take time and effort. Don't get discouraged when your numbers aren't going up the way you want them to.

Be authentic

It's important to remain authentic with your audience. If you are fake, sooner or later people are going to see through you and you won't have a very big or engaged audience for long. Don't forget to share your story with your audience as well. People love to hear how other people got started on their entrepreneurial journey.

You should also be consistent with your audience both online and offline. Your audience should feel that you are reliable in both your uploading schedule and your online personality.

Connecting with your community

In the process of building your community and after you have built up a really good following, you can't forget to connect with your community.

It's very important to connect with your audience, it not only benefits you as a creator but also benefits your community. Here are a few ways to connect with your audience:

Have conversations in the comments section

Remember when I mentioned before that you should comment on your own videos? This is not only a good practice to boost your videos but also to ask people to engage in the comments section. Make sure that you are promoting quality conversations in the comments section (Uhas, 2019) and responding to viewers' comments within the first few hours of them being posted. This lets viewers know that you care about their comments and appreciate that they are watching your videos. But make sure that you are only responding to actual comments that are meaningful and add value; don't respond to negative comments. Interacting with your audience in the comments section can also benefit you by providing useful information or suggestions and ideas for future videos.

Just as you would engage in the comments by commenting back, make full use of YouTube's tools and heart peoples' comments as well. This will, in turn, send them a notification letting them know that you have "hearted" their comments and that you, again, appreciate their contribution to your channel. Hearting a comment is something only the creator is allowed to do and shows a little something extra to your viewers.

Another really neat thing you can do in the comments section of your videos is to pin a comment to the top of the comments section. This allows for better engagement when you are asking your audience questions during your actual video. Your username in the comments is also surrounded by a little bubble of color, which helps to quickly indicate that you are an engaged creator.

Ask your audience for feedback

It's a great idea to also ask your audience for feedback. You don't have to worry about having a ton of views on your videos before you do this either. Pin a comment at the top of the comments section asking what your audience would like to see in upcoming videos. You can also do shout-outs to your audience in your videos. For example, "Today's video idea came from [viewer name]." This really helps to make your audience feel extra special and that you are really engaging with them.

There are a couple different ways that people can be notified of activity on your channel: by subscribing and by hitting the notifications bell. When they hit the notifications bell they are notified whenever you upload a new video.

Reward your superfans

There are two really fun ways that you can reward your superfans, those that watch EVERYTHING you put out and comment on all of your videos. You can make private videos or do livestreams. As a full-time RVer you could live stream taking your super audience on special adventures with you. This is also a great way to encourage regular audience members to become super members by bribing them with exclusive content.

Connect off of YouTube

Just because you are building a YouTube channel doesn't mean that you just have to stay on the YouTube platform. I previously mentioned being able to connect with other creators and your potential audience on other social media platforms. When you are first starting out and learning the ropes of everything, it is ok to stick to one channel. As your channel grows, expand your reach by using other social media channels.

The first thing to start with is promoting your videos on your other social media networks. Don't be afraid to do this a few times per week per video you are putting out. Videos that do really well on social media are the kinds of videos that are often funny, inspirational, or things that are very "Buzzfeed" inspired. So keep that in mind when you are creating your videos and sharing them on your various social media platforms.

Documenting your RV adventures for your subscribers

Think about this for a minute, if you have the dream of traveling around full time in an RV, do you watch videos on YouTube that inspire you or provide you with information on full-time RV living? I'm guessing you have watched at least a few. People love watching what others are doing and how they are achieving success and living their dreams. They find it inspirational as well as motivational.

Even if you start your YouTube channel before you officially start your RV adventure, there is no rule saying that you can only have one channel! People LOVE to watch videos on travel and traveling-tips. If you initially start a YouTube channel about something else, it is also a great idea to be able to document your RV adventures. Just do a quick search on "RV living" on YouTube and you can come up with a whole list of topics:

- RV remodels
- How much it really costs
- How to budget while being a full-time RVer

- Beginner mistakes that RVers make
- RV tours

Videos like these are getting TONS of views! So you can already see that there is an audience out there watching these videos.

GETTING PAID-ACTIVE AND PASSIVE INCOME IDEAS

While the goal of starting your YouTube channel is to make money, it is going to take a little bit to make that happen. Before you can start collecting checks from YouTube, you need to build an audience and make consistent content. Once you have a consistent stream of content and you are building up your audience, you can apply to the YouTube Partner Program to start actually monetizing your content. There are a couple of requirements that you need to meet before you can be accepted to the YouTube Partner Program:

- You need to be in good standing with YouTube
- Have at least 4,000 valid watch hours
- Have at least 1,000 subscribers

While this might sound like some big milestones to get started, if you follow the aforementioned tactics, you should be able to reach those milestones pretty quickly! However, it can take up to a month for YouTube to actually review and approve your channel, so keep that in mind. If for whatever reason your channel doesn't get approved, then you can reapply again in 30 days. In the meantime, read through YouTube's policies and see if there is something that you need to change in order to get approved. One of the main reasons that creators get removed from the Partner Program is if they are inactive for 6 months and fall below the qualification thresholds.

How you can actually generate revenue from ads

Once you have officially qualified for the YouTube Partner Program you can start to earn money from ads and from YouTube premium subscribers.

Ads are one of the most common ways that people make money on YouTube, specifically because there is a lower threshold to be able to make money from ads than from any other monetization strategy. But HOW you can make money from ads can be sort of confusing when you are just getting started.

After you have ensured that your content is advertiser friendly, you need to physically turn on ads on the platform. While YouTube does most of the heavy lifting when it comes to determining what type of ads are shown on your videos, there are a few ways that you can ensure that your audience will see relevant ads. YouTube determines which ads to put on videos based on your audience, the video-metadata, and if it is advertiser friendly.

There are several different kinds of ads that your videos can have. Display ads are shown to the right of your video and above the list of suggested videos. Overlay ads lay over the bottom 20% of the video that are semi-transparent. Bumper ads are those that the viewer can not skip and must watch the full ad before your video plays. There are also, of course, skippable ads as well as sponsored content that is relevant to your video. Finally, if your video is longer, there are mid-roll ads which play in the middle of the video.

Additional ways to earn money through YouTube

Recently, YouTube has been rolling out some new features for creators to earn additional income streams from their channels, such as memberships and super chat.

Memberships

YouTube memberships are only available for creators that have 100,000 subscribers and are over the age of 18 (sorry, no kids channels), and have already qualified for the YouTube Partner Program. Members can pay $4.99 per month to support the channel and get additional perks like badges and access to exclusive content in the community area of the channel.

Merchandise

YouTube has also added a merchandise feature. This is great news for creators as this can really help to increase their earnings. If the channel has 10,000 subscribers or more, YouTube creators can offer merchandise that shows up in a strip below their videos.

While there is really unlimited potential to this avenue, as a creator you should offer products that make sense to your audience. T-shirts are always a good place to start! *Hint: this is also why you should always create a brand from the beginning! YouTube has actually developed a partnership with TeeSpring to help initiate those sales. While obviously YouTube and TeeSpring have to take a cut of the sales, there is still plenty to be made.

Sponsorships

Creators can also land sponsored opportunities through FameBit.com. Sponsored opportunities are a great way to earn extra income on YouTube by connecting with much larger companies and promoting their products or services.

One really neat way to calculate how much money you can actually make from YouTube is to use the YouTube Money Calculator. You can also plug in a channel and it will show you approximately how much that channel is making. Just remember that you, the creator, only receive 55% of that total and you still need to pay taxes on those earnings as well. So if you live in the United States, take about another 30% away from your total. So out of every $100 you "make" on YouTube you only get to keep approximately $38.50.

What you need to know about YouTube ads

I've mentioned a few times about creating content that is advertiser-friendly, but what does this actually mean? First of all, what you need to realize is that not every video uploaded to YouTube is manually reviewed but rather initially reviewed by an algorithm. Sometimes this algorithm doesn't have enough information from the video for it to determine if it adheres to YouTube's advertiser friendly guidelines. In this case, it might get demonetized.

But fear not!

You can always request a manual review if you feel that you are adhering to the guidelines. The thumbnail, description, and the title of your video can have a huge impact. It should not have any swear words, anything racy, and the thumbnail, description, and title should all be directly relevant to the video itself.

What NOT to make videos about

Some of the topics that advertisers find off-limits are issues such as school shootings, terrorism, death, sexual abuse, and any kind of related topics. The bottom line is you can certainly make videos on these topics, but many advertisers just don't want to be associated with those kinds of topics, therefore those types of videos will likely be demonetized.

Topics that revolve around drugs or substance abuse can be monetized but ONLY if they are education-based and not promoting the use, abuse, or sale of such substances. Advertisers can also choose to be shown on videos that include potentially sensitive drug material.

Videos that also include potentially physical and emotional harm to another person can also be a little iffy as to whether they are able to be monetized. Prank videos are a perfect example of this. While prank videos can certainly be monetized, and many people make a good living doing these types of videos, it should be shown in the video that the individual that is getting pranked is not seriously injured.

Swearing and profanity can be a big cause of having videos demonetized. While it is certainly ok to drop a swear word here and there in your videos, bleep them if possible. Leave them out of the title, description, and thumbnail. The context of the swearing also has a lot to do with whether or not your videos will be monetized or not. If it is mean-spirited, then it is likely that your video will be flagged. However, if you are saying it as a reaction to something then that is generally acceptable.

Realistically, there are various kinds of content that advertisers don't want their ads running on. If you are unsure if your content is advertiser-friendly, you can always reference YouTube's Advertiser-Friendly Guidelines. This goes into the various different categories that advertisers don't want their ads running on as well as limited ads based on the nature of the content.

CHAPTER SUMMARY

Getting started with YouTube is very easy. You don't need anything other than a smartphone camera and a computer to start your channel.

Make sure to do your research and take a look at other popular channels in the same niche and what kind of content they are creating.

Don't be afraid to mess up. Start with what you have, use natural light whenever possible. If you are looking at video equipment, take the smaller size of an RV into consideration before making your purchase.

Come up with a consistent content schedule for recording, editing, and uploading.

Again, try not to be a perfectionist here. It's better to create your content with a less than perfect setup and get it out there than to not do anything at all.

Give your video an initial boose by commenting, liking, and sharing it on other platforms. This also helps to increase your social proof, so the more views it has, the more views it will get.

Consistency is key! Be consistent in uploading your videos even though it might take six to twelve months to see the growth you desire.

Often an overlooked aspect to driving growth on your channel is to actually ask people to like, subscribe, and hit the notifications bell.

Grow your channel through collaborating with other YouTubers and influencers. Always make sure that you are providing your viewers with high quality and valuable content.

Connect with your audience through the comments section, asking for feedback, and by rewarding your superfans. You can also connect with your audience outside of YouTube on other social media platforms like Facebook and Twitter.

While you can certainly start a channel about something else before you start out on your RV adventures, there is nothing wrong with having two channels.

Make sure that you understand all of YouTube's policies so that you are more likely to get approved to monetize using ads. YouTube does all the heavy lifting when it comes to which ads to run on your videos.

YouTube creators can also earn money through memberships and merchandise when they meet additional qualifications. Creators can also work with sponsors to create additional revenue streams.

You should always make sure that you are adhering to YouTube's advertiser guidelines so you can continue to monetize your videos. In order for your videos to remain monetized, ensure that you stay away from topics that involve drugs, sex, school shootings, terrorism, sexual abuse, physical violence, death, profanity, and all that other bad stuff.

CHAPTER RESOURCES

Video editors

- iMovie
- Windows Movie Creator
- Filmora

YouTube resources

- FameBit.com - for sponsorship opportunities
- YouTube Money Calculator - check out how much your favorite channels are making!
- YouTube's Advertiser-Friendly Guidelines

In the next chapter, we are going to cover how to build a sustainable business using affiliate marketing.

CHAPTER SIX
The Secrets To Affiliate Marketing Only The Pros Know

A FFILIATE MARKETING IS a great way to start your online journey. There are hundreds, if not thousands of online millionaires that either started as affiliate marketers or are still doing affiliate marketing, at least in some capacity.

There are also some very good opportunities to earn affiliate commissions on a passive income basis.

In this chapter, we are going to take a look at what affiliate marketing actually is, the best companies to use to start your affiliate marketing journey, how affiliate marketers earn money, why it's easier to sell other people's products, and if you need a website to get started!

WHAT IS AFFILIATE MARKETING?

Some of the biggest names in online business got started with affiliate marketing and learning how to generate passive income.

The Golden Goose, the American Dream...

To make money while you sleep!

The basic premise of affiliate marketing is that you promote other peoples' products and earn a commission when someone buys a product through your link. Sounds pretty easy right?

Within the affiliate marketing model there are three main components: the advertiser, the publisher, and the customer. The advertiser is the person or company whose products you are promoting. As an affiliate marketer, you are the publisher. Finally, the customer is just that, the person who is buying the product or service.

As an affiliate, it is your job to convince the customer to buy the product or service so that you get paid a commission. But the customer actually needs to buy something in order for that to happen. You can promote affiliate offers through your own review website, social networks, email marketing, or even ads (if that is ok with the advertiser). The great thing about affiliate marketing is that the price of the actual products or services doesn't increase just because the affiliate is earning a commission.

You can find merchants or advertisers either through affiliate networks or as an individual company or solopreneur. Affiliate networks offer a wide range of affiliate products to choose from, often from many different categories. Some merchants choose only to go through an affiliate network to manage their affiliates.

You can also become an affiliate for more than one company. Then there are the affiliate programs for solopreneurs or other small business owners. This often includes being an affiliate for a limited number of products, such as the creator's course or ebook.

It really doesn't matter what niche you want to cover, there is a related affiliate program out there to promote. There are thousands of affiliate products for B2B and B2C. By far, one of the biggest and most well known affiliate programs out there is the Amazon Associates program. It is easy to apply to and you don't even need a website to get accepted.

THE BEST AFFILIATE COMPANIES TO JOIN

There are thousands, if not millions of affiliate programs that you could join. But the good news is that you don't need to worry about joining a thousand different affiliate programs. There is one in particular that does a great job for just about any niche you are in, as well as a few really good runner ups.

Amazon Associates

Amazon is the best affiliate program to join when you are first starting out. Not only is Amazon Associates great for those that are just starting out, huge companies like Buzzfeed and the New York Times use Amazon's affiliate program to monetize their sites. In the United States alone, 49% of ALL online sales can be attributed to Amazon. That is HUGE!

People are making hundreds and thousands of dollars per month just from the Amazon Associates program and there doesn't seem to be any slowing down.

Bloggers and business owners love using the Amazon Associates program for many reasons. One of the biggest things is that Amazon is so big that you can find just about any product on there that will fit in with your niche.

From baby products to some pretty weird and crazy stuff like a bag of air (seriously, I'm not even joking about this!), there are bound to be products in your niche. Even better, more than likely, you are bound to find something that your audience will want to buy. Amazon is also pretty old in internet terms, which is a good thing. It has such an incredible knowledge of its customers and gets an insane amount of traffic every day.

There are, however, a couple of downfalls about the Amazon Associates program to take into consideration.

First, it is mostly for physical products, other than eBooks. So if you are looking to promote other people's digital programs, Amazon can't help much with that, although who knows what the future will bring. If you want to promote a mix of both physical and digital products you can supplement your Amazon affiliate income with Clickbank products.

Amazon can also be pretty strict, which can make it difficult for some people to follow their terms of service. Just make sure that you are thoroughly reading Amazon's Terms of Service and under-standing them so you don't get yourself into trouble.

While you can make a lot from Amazon, there are some niches where commissions are much lower than others, so take that into account when you are picking which products to promote.

There are a ton of benefits to using the Amazon Associates program. We already know how big it is and just about everyone has heard of Amazon. This means the trust factor is already there and you don't have to worry about convincing people to buy. Because of the trust factor, the conversions for Amazon are pretty high. There are tons of different ways in which you can promote Amazon affiliate products.

Lastly, you have the option to transition to the Amazon FBA program (more on this in the next chapter). Amazon has also become a master at upselling their customers, which benefits you as you earn a commission on anything that customer buys within 24 hours after clicking on your link.

HOW EXACTLY DO AFFILIATES EARN MONEY?

Amazon is a little different than other affiliate programs out there. Similar to other programs, when someone clicks on your link and are taken to the Amazon site, they are tagged with your special code that attributes the sale (and commission) to you. The neat thing about the Amazon Associates program is that once they click on your link, whatever they buy from Amazon in the next 24 hours, you get a commission for. This means, if they click your link to buy a $2.99 eBook, and then decide to purchase a new $800 tv within the next 24 hours, you get the commission.

There are several ways that you can earn money from Amazon by promoting their products. If you are recommending a certain product, you simply link the product. You can do this by talking about the product in a blog post and simply linking to it through what is called an anchor text. This simply means that you use keywords of the product in the text and link to the product.

You can also use what are called native shopping ads. You can create these native ads, which look like other regular ads, for individual products within categories of products. This is great to use to stack on top of other Amazon revenue streams. For example, if you are making a post about Instant Pot recipes, you can place a native ad in the post that links to certain Instant Pot accessories.

Did you know that 60% of Amazon's sales come from mobile users? Which is why mobile popover ads can be so beneficial to add Amazon revenue to your passive income streams.

Once someone has clicked on your link and been taken to Amazon, they make a purchase. In order for you to get a payout, the purchase needs to be completed and delivered. If they make a return, you don't get a commission.

You can get paid out via direct deposit with as little as $10, or if you prefer old fashioned checks, then you have to wait until you have accumulated at least $100 in affiliate commissions. Depending on the product, you can earn between 1%-10% affiliate commission on products. There are certain things that don't pay out a commission either, such as gift cards, wireless service plans, digital Kindle products, alcoholic beverages, and a few others.

The actual sign up process is super simple and only takes a few minutes. Almost anyone can easily get approved to start promoting affiliate products through Amazon.

Getting people to click on your links

So you know how to get links to products and use ads to promote Amazon products, but what about actually getting people to click on your links? It's not as complicated as it sounds. There are a couple of different ways to promote your Amazon links and start earning an income from them!

If you already have a blog or are thinking of starting one, then roundup posts are a great place to start putting in your affiliate links. You have most likely already seen these online and have read a few of them yourself. These types of posts often target "the best" kinds of products to drive sales of the product.

When writing a roundup post, be careful though, Amazon is very particular about how much of their content you can use within your post. For example, you should not use their ratings but rather ensure that your reader knows that the ratings you are including (if you are including ratings) are all your own opinion.

A traditional roundup is meant to act as a buying guide to help customers make informed buying decisions. Including product reviews can be very helpful here. But again, watch out when you are taking information from Amazon. Don't just use the product description but rather share with your readers why you are recommending the product to them.

There are also roundup listicles, which are very similar to the traditional roundup post. Roundup listicles are more shopper-centric and are easier for readers to browse without having to read too much if they don't want to. These often link to the Amazon full reviews rather than reviewing the product itself. The big downfall with this is that smaller sites shouldn't do it. Google doesn't exactly like sites that are JUST affiliate links and no actual education or information for the reader.

The last kind of roundup that is great for promoting your affiliate links is the "clear winner" roundup. This helps to take some of the guesswork out of which product the buyer should purchase by giving them a "clear winner" or "editor's choice." While this is technically a roundup post, most of the content will focus on the best product (*Hint, which is often the most expensive one, which gets you a higher commission) while briefly mentioning other, comparable products.

Then there are single product reviews. These are just a post on a review of a single product rather than several. The great thing about roundups and product reviews is that there is buying intent behind these searches. It all comes down to the psychology of sales.

Think for a minute, before you make a purchase, often a larger purchase, you might look for product reviews to determine which product to purchase. Think of keyword phrases like "the best running shoes," or "the best recumbent bikes," generally speaking if you are looking up phrases like these then you are about ready to buy something rather than just doing more research. With writing a single product review you need to go into a little more depth on the actual product and not just rehash some information from Amazon.

A versus post is taking two products and comparing the pros and cons to each other. Rather than giving your readers only one choice, or a whole host of options, they only have to choose between two options. This can be very helpful for those that are rather indecisive.

People often do this comparison by themselves anyways. When they have narrowed down on their search results and have picked two products but can't seem to decide on one or the other they will often search "[product A] versus [product b]." If they can find a post of exactly the two products they are looking for that will help to build trust in that source, which is you.

Finally, there are tutorials and problem solving content. Generally speaking, there is urgency associated with someone looking online for a tutorial or something to help them solve an issue. When someone is in need of something to help them solve a problem this can drastically help with conversions as well.

Often times tutorial type posts don't even need to focus on the product that much and can just provide it as a solution to the audience. Think of posts that start with things like: "*The benefits of...*," "*How to...*," and "*X# of ways to...*"

You can easily put in Amazon affiliate links into any post by searching Amazon and using the Site Stripe once you have signed up for a business account. The Site Stripe is just a bar that goes across the top of your Amazon business account. Once you type in a product and click on the individual product you can link via a short link, a long link, using just an image, or using an image and text.

It is recommended that you do use the full affiliate link rather than the shortened version, this can assist in making the transition to change the links in the future much easier.

There are also several other ways to build links from Amazon into your website or blog, which include the Amazon Publisher Studio, the Amazon Link Builder Plugin for WordPress, and OneLink. All of these offer their own advantages and can be used to easily change links should the need arise.

While there are plenty of places where you can promote Amazon affiliate links, there are places in which you can not. Doing so will likely get your account deleted and there goes all of your commissions along with it! Here are a few things that you need to make sure you have in place and that you DON'T do when you are trying to earn money through Amazon affiliate links.

- Always have a disclaimer on your site.

This can be either on each individual post, in the footer, or sidebar. But you need to make sure that it is very clear to your audience that you earn a commission from Amazon if someone makes a purchase through your link.

- Don't download images from Amazon and use them on your site.

This is a big no-no! If you reference Amazon's Terms of Service, the wording on this is sort of vague. But it is always better to err on the side of caution when it comes to using images. You can, however, use the images that are available through the Site Stripe.

- Whatever Amazon images you do use MUST link back to the product on Amazon.
- You can not promote Amazon products via email.

This does not mean that you can't write a post about a product and link to that post within the email. Again, better safe than sorry here.

- You can not promote any Amazon products by using pop-up ads.
- You can't put the price out there.

Unfortunately, many people still do this and are unknowingly violating the Terms of Service. For example, if you are promoting a product you can not place a button under it stating the price. You can, however, place a button that says something like, *"Click here to check price,"* or *"Buy Now,"* or *"Check Amazon for Lowest Price."* These are all great options that still encourage people to click through without violating the Terms of Service. The only time that you can directly mention the price of an item on Amazon is when you link to the API. This helps to pull the most recent price directly from Amazon so you aren't intentionally or unintentionally misleading your customers with a false price. You can also use vague dollar symbols in place of actual prices.

- Don't try and get your friends and family to buy stuff through your links.

Amazon is SMART! They can tell if you are just sending people links to get them to buy stuff so you can generate a commission. This is one sure way to get your account shut down. Customers must click on your link through a natural buying process and can't be forced.

- You can share your links on social media.

The only stipulation is that you need to add your social media profiles to your list of approved sites with Amazon. Then you are good to go!

Other Affiliate Networks to Consider

In addition to using Amazon as an affiliate platform there are a few others that are worth considering:

- Clickbank-Great for digital products in a wide variety of niches.
- Rakuten-Affiliate platform for places like Target, Walmart, and Kohl's.
- eBay Partner Program-for everything available on eBay!
- ShareASale-Great if you are planning on doing B2B, lots of business-related products.
- FlexOffers-Some featured advertisers include CreditSesame and Overstock.com.

- GiddyUp-This is a great platform for those affiliates that are looking to get into highly specific or more obscure niches.
- JVZoo-This program offers a lot of software-based and digital products.
- CJ Affiliate by Conversant-A HUGE name in affiliate marketing, some of their advertisers include GoPro, Barnes and Noble, and Priceline.
- Avangate-A great option if you want to promote software products (Edwards, 2018).
- MarketHealth-Great for health and beauty products.

While some offers are only available on certain affiliate platforms, there are some businesses that are affiliated through multiple platforms. In this case, make sure to do your research to see which one pays out higher commissions or has more affiliate resources. Heck, some affiliate platforms even let you become an affiliate, meaning that if someone becomes an affiliate for that platform you can then make money off of their commissions too!

One thing to keep in mind when you are choosing which affiliate network to start working with is that digital and software products often have higher commission payouts than physical products.

WHY IT'S BETTER TO SELL OTHER PEOPLE'S PRODUCTS

While Amazon is a great affiliate platform to use, wouldn't you make more money if you just made your own products?

Well, yes and no...

You could certainly spend months developing a product, working with suppliers from overseas, creating an entire marketing plan around your ONE product.

OR...

You would simply hook up with other merchants and use their products. This is a lot less work on your part and you can start generating cash a lot quicker and with a lot less investment in both time and money.

While creating your own product can be highly profitable, it can be rather pricey and labor intensive to get started. When you use other people's products there is already proven success that people buy those products, otherwise they probably wouldn't be on Amazon in the first place.

With many kinds of affiliates, they often have full campaigns in place. This can include product landing pages, email newsletter templates, video sales letters, and long-form sales letters that these companies often pay hundreds of thousands of dollars to initially get set up.

So it is not only free for you to start making money through affiliate links, there is a whole host of resources that you are able to use to help drive sales. The more sales you are able to drive to the product, the more money you make, and the more money the merchant makes. It's really a win-win for everyone involved.

DO YOU ACTUALLY NEED A WEBSITE TO BE AN AFFILIATE?

There are plenty of affiliates who got their start without a website. However, there is a lot more you can do if you have your own site. It can vary drastically from merchant to merchant and from network to network. Some affiliate networks won't even let you sign up if you don't already have a website that has content that they can approve.

Let's take Amazon and Clickbank for example. You don't technically need a website to share affiliate links. You can "microblog," simply meaning that you are putting an affiliate link in a very small post on social media in order to promote it.

Some other affiliate networks will require you to have a website, such as FlexOffers. Often times this helps merchants to see how you will be promoting their products. Even if you are accepted into an affiliate network, you might also need to apply to every individual merchant. If for whatever reason you get denied, there should be an explanation in which you can work to resolve the issue and apply again for approval.

The biggest piece of advice that I have when it comes to affiliate marketing is to choose one niche to focus on. It can be very tempting when you see the potential to make a lot of money from all the different affiliate networks out there to want to do them all. Do your best to avoid shiny object syndrome and focus on one, at least in the beginning.

Affiliate marketing is also a great passive income tool. There are so many things that you can outsource and automate once you get your systems up and running. Of course, the more passive income you are able to generate the better!

CHAPTER SUMMARY

Many online millionaires have started their journey with affiliate marketing. Affiliate marketing is also a great passive income model.

The basic idea of affiliate marketing is that you set up a site or put links out online and when people buy through those links you earn a commission.

In an affiliate marketing relationship there is the advertizer, the publisher (that's you), and the customer. You can promote affiliate links through your website, social media accounts, email list, and even ads. You earn a commission all while the customer does not have to worry about a price increase.

There are many different affiliate platforms and marketplaces to choose from. Be sure to understand each program's terms of service.

Amazon pays you a commission on everything the customer buys within 24 hours of clicking on your link. You can earn a commission from Amazon through affiliate links, native shopping ads, and mobile pop over ads.

You can drive traffic to your links through roundup posts, review posts, buying guides, and roundup listicles. Make sure you are not just filling your site with affiliate links and that it has some educational content as well.

When you are writing your post, keep the buyer intent in mind. When linking to Amazon products, it is recommended to use the full link rather than the shortened version.

There are a few things that you need to make sure that you do (and don't do) when promoting Amazon affiliate links:

- Have a disclaimer on your site.
- Don't use images directly from Amazon.
- You can use Site Stripe images.
- Any image should link back to the Amazon product.
- You can't promote products directly through email.
- You can't use pop-up ads.
- You can't advertise the price unless linked with API.
- Don't bribe your friends and family to buy stuff through your links.
- You can share your links on social media.

Digital and software products often have higher payouts than physical products. It is also a lot easier to get started selling other peoples' products than to start off selling your own.

There are many affiliate networks available that you don't even need a website to get started with.

CHAPTER RESOURCES

Affiliate companies/platforms

- Amazon Associates
- Clickbank
- Rakuten
- eBay Partner Program
- ShareASale
- FlexOffers
- GiddyUp
- JVZoo
- CJ Affiliate by Conversant
- Avangate
- MarketHealth

In the next chapter, we are going to cover the essentials you need to successfully start an Amazon FBA business.

CHAPTER SEVEN
Essential Amazon FBA Tactics To Grow Your Business

D ID YOU KNOW that there are over 2 million people selling products on Amazon? You might not realize it but Amazon is very similar to eBay in that just about anyone can list things for sale on Amazon. It doesn't matter if you purchased the item wholesale, made it yourself, or it was something you were going to put in a garage sale.

In this chapter, we are going to cover all the essentials of getting started with Amazon FBA. This includes what FBA actually is, how you can select a winning product or products that people are willing to pay for, where to find these products, how FBAs actually make money, and how to run Amazon ads to drive traffic to your products.

WHAT IS AMAZON FBA?

While you can fulfill orders you receive on Amazon personally, there is an easier way, especially if you have a lot of products. This is where Amazon FBA, or Fulfillment By Amazon, comes in really handy! You can get your product, ship it to Amazon, they keep it stored in their warehouse, and they will take care of the rest. This includes packing, shipping, and even returns.

You can see why so many people find this to be an attractive business model.

This is particularly attractive to someone living the RV lifestyle as you don't have to worry about carting around inventory, packing materials, or finding the nearest UPS to ship out your orders.

Once all the initial leg work is done, there is a lot less to worry about on a regular basis than if you were personally handling all of the orders.

One of the advantages of selling on Amazon through FBA is that your products are available for Amazon Prime. Considering Amazon Prime members spend almost twice the amount annually on Amazon purchases, there is a huge market of buyers just waiting to purchase your product(s).

In addition to handling pretty much everything once Amazon receives your products (there sometimes might be minimal customer service involved), you get paid every two weeks! No having to wait three months before ever seeing a check. As long as you are making sales, this creates reliable and consistent income, which is great when you are living on the road!

Starting your FBA business

So what does it take to get set up with Amazon FBA anyhow?

It does take some work to get started selling on Amazon through FBA. First, you need to choose a product to sell - sometimes this is easier said than done. This is where a lot of people get hung up and quit before they ever even get started.

We will focus on how to pick a winning product in the next section.

If you are going to be using FBA (which is the goal here!) then pick a product that is going to sell fast. This way you are turning a profit quickly and won't have to worry about paying Amazon storage fees.

The next step is to keep your inventory stocked. While this is a simple task, it is very important. If you are constantly running out of stock you are going to lose customers and Amazon will be less likely to show your listing to potential customers.

Lastly, and this is the biggest upkeep part, is the advertising and marketing of your products. With hundreds of millions of products on Amazon you need to be sure that your product doesn't get buried and people actually see it and buy it.

The challenges and benefits of Amazon FBA

If you are leaning towards starting an Amazon FBA business, there are some things to take into consideration before you jump in feet first.

It can cost a bit to get started with Amazon FBA. In addition to paying for the actual products, which can cost thousands of dollars initially, there are Amazon service fees and fulfilment fees.

There is also the potential to pay storage fees if your inventory sits in the warehouse for too long. Amazon wants to sell your products just as much as you do, however, if your products are sitting in their warehouse for six-months or more, you are going to be charged a pretty penny for it.

While having Amazon Prime is great and it can make returns for customers super easy, that isn't always good for you. Making things easy to return means that impulse buys are more likely to be returned; it happens. After awhile you should be able to see a trend in your product sales and returns and be able to predict your potential loss for returns.

Amazon is a well oiled machine for a reason, they are very particular with how they want things done. You need to have your items properly prepared and shipped to the right warehouse. While this might take some time to get the hang of, once you know how to do it, it shouldn't be very difficult.

As I said before, you need to be able to keep up on your inventory so you don't run out and lose customers. It can be difficult to track inventory and sync everything up. However, there are automated apps and software that help to alleviate this annoyance.

And then there are taxes...

Nobody likes taxes, they are a pain in the butt, and vary by state and country. But again, there are solutions to help automate the tax process so you don't get hung up with this.

The benefits of selling through Amazon FBA

While there certainly is a learning curve with Amazon FBA, and it can be rather intimidating for people to get started, there are certainly numerous benefits!

There are so many amazing things about selling through Amazon FBA. Without having to manage your own fulfillment you can save a ton of time and stress. Having to fill your own orders is very time consuming, not to mention, takes up a lot of space, which you don't have if you are living full-time in an RV. If you are selling a lot of products, that means more space you need and more time spent fulfilling the orders.

You don't have to worry about outrageous shipping costs either. Amazon has partnered with some of the biggest shipping carriers to offer its FBA members a huge discount on shipping costs (Carragher, 2018). The customer benefits also as there as several ways to get free shipping, such as through a Prime membership as well as purchasing qualified items, generally spending $25 or more.

Amazon FBA also handles all of your returns. Amazon handles everything, for a small processing fee. This can include handling upset customers, all the admin tasks that go along with it, customer inquiries, return and shipping labels, 24-hour customer phone support, and so on. While there is a charge for this, it is definitely worth it to make your business more passive.

Unlike other businesses that require certain amounts of inventory, there is no minimum for Amazon FBA, you can even send them just one product. You also pretty much have unlimited storage potential. This is great news if you are just testing the waters, and also if you are rapidly expanding. And the best part? You don't have to worry about your inventory taking up any space in your RV!

With Amazon's nationwide reach, there should be no problem getting customers their products quickly. Now, some Prime members can get their products in a day! Amazon also offers Multi-Channel Fulfillment, which means that you can sell your Amazon product on other platforms, such as BigCommerce, and Amazon will still work to fulfill those orders, pretty neat!

HOW TO SELECT WINNING PRODUCTS THAT SELL!

This is another area where people can really get hung up. They realize that they NEED products to sell. They might have an idea as to what to sell. However, they can be so overwhelmed at the same time that they end up picking the wrong thing or never even bother getting started.

There are literally millions of things that you could choose to sell online, from sponges to supplements and everything in between. While many people can handle figuring out the logistics and the marketing aspects of Amazon FBA, the part of the business that includes picking out a product to sell is downright scary! What if you pick the wrong thing? What if it doesn't sell? What if the market is too saturated?

Believe me, everyone that started Amazon FBA has had the same fears and questions. The difference between people that consistently doubt themselves and the ones that actually make a good living online doing Amazon FBA is confidence!

Once they have chosen their products, they are confident in their sales process that they are going to make enough money to support themselves and their business. While picking the wrong product can waste you a lot of time and money (which nobody wants) picking a product that sells can help to exponentially grow your business.

While products themselves are important, the niche(s) you pick to promote hold just as much clout. People often think that they have to start with picking a product before they pick a niche, this is simply not true. You should pick a niche before you dive into product research.

Even with really good research and picking a profitable niche, it is likely that your first product won't be a total hit. There is a lot of trial and error when it comes to Amazon FBA.

When it comes to picking a niche, it is better to go narrower than wider. As the saying goes, the riches are in the niches. The great thing about hyper-focused niches in that the customers in those niches are super passionate. Take road biking for example. While there are lots of people that like to ride their bikes, road biking or cycling is a hyper-focused niche. Cyclists spend a lot of money on their bikes and accessories. Amazon does a great job of catering to this by placing their products in categories, which gives you an advantage for finding a niche (Bryant, 2014). Here is an example of what I mean:

Home, Garden & Pets > Pet Supplies > Houses & Habitats > Accessories > Aquarium Décor > Plastic Plants

Your niche then would be aquarium decor and or plastic plants.

Now that you have a general idea on how to pick a product, what about *actually* picking a product? If you have some ideas on products you would like to sell but still aren't sure where to start, JungleScout is your best option. JungleScout is a software and Chrome browser extension that will help you to pick winning products over and over again! JungleScout can help you to find profitable products, track product sales, get details on Amazon search data, research quality suppliers, improve your advertising campaigns, optimize your listings to increase buyers, launch new products, and send automated emails to your customers. In addition, with the Chrome browser extension, you can get an insight into instant sales estimates, evaluate a product's revenue potential, validate product demand, and analyze the competition. Basically, if you aren't using JungleScout to help you run your Amazon FBA business, you are leaving a lot to chance.

WHERE CAN I FIND PRODUCTS TO SOURCE?

The vast majority of people first getting started with Amazon FBA start by importing their products from China. The biggest reason for this is because they are cheap and the profit margins are generally higher. However, there is a rather large learning curve that goes along with importing from overseas.

The two most common sites to use to import products from China are Alibaba and AliExpress. Aliexpress is great if you just want to order a few different products to get started with to test the waters without having to commit to a larger wholesale orders. You can order even one product at a time to get a feel for the quality and customer service when working with China wholesalers.

Alibaba, on the other hand, you have to place wholesale orders with. While some minimum orders can be as small as two pieces, there are many that require you to order hundreds of pieces of product at a time. When placing a wholesale order with Alibaba, you will also receive a discount on pricing the more you order. While this is generally a few cents per unit, that can really add up when you are ordering hundreds of units.

When you begin working with a supplier, you should ask for samples to ensure that you are getting a good quality product. Most often, suppliers are more than willing to work with a buyer (that's you) to provide you with a product that you will keep buying from them. Suppliers can also alter products to your specifications, such as creating different colors or adding your logo on the product to make it stand out from the millions of other products on Amazon.

It is better to go through a few rounds of samples to ensure you are getting exactly what you want rather than worrying about upsetting the supplier and having to pay for a huge order that is going to get bad reviews.

Why you should outsource from overseas

Other than generating high profit margins, there are several other reasons why you should consider placing your wholesale orders from a wholesaler in China.

It is actually very easy to import items from China to America. With some items it is actually cheaper to ship from China to the U.S. rather than to ship within the U.S. This is because the U.S. Postal Service and China sellers actually have deals to highly cut the cost of shipping items that are under one pound.

You don't have to worry about traveling to China to see your products that you are selling (Bryant, 2018), although you certainly can travel to China. *Bonus-that's a tax deduction! So why not go see your products and the wholesaler factory up close and personal while also enjoying a fun and relaxing vacation?

When you are working with wholesalers in China, you don't have to settle for standard off-the-shelf products. You can actually work with them to develop a product from scratch or improve upon an existing product. Being able to actually develop a real, tangible product from scratch is fun and exciting. Even if it's a small product, there really isn't anything better than holding that real product in your hands for the first time!

While you might think that you are too late to the game, don't worry, you aren't!

Amazon has been growing and will continue to grow in the future. Just look around you. How many stores, even larger chains, close their doors because they haven't been getting enough business? The trend of online shopping isn't going to be slowing down any time soon. People are always looking for new products and ways to improve their lives with things they buy on Amazon.

While this might sound like an expensive endeavor, it is what you make of it. Many people have started their Amazon FBA businesses with only a few hundred dollars. Although it is ideal to be able to start with a few thousand dollars to allow for a little more wiggle room with testing. You must also have an Amazon Seller Central account which will cost you about $40 a month.

A word of caution though.

You should look into becoming an LLC rather than just a sole proprietor. Whenever you are dealing with products, there is always the potential for something to go wrong. A kid could swallow something, customers could misuse the product and somehow become injured. It happens. If you are a sole proprietor you can personally be sued for damages and lose everything that you have built.

However, if you establish an LLC, you personally can not he held liable for any damages. You are then a separate entity from your business. So take this into consideration when you are budgeting everything when starting out.

CASHING IN: HOW TO MAKE MONEY WITH AMAZON FBA

Now that we have covered what it takes and how much it costs to get started, it's time to talk about what everyone wants to know. How much money can you make with Amazon FBA.

The short answer is…

There is no guarantee. There are two main things to consider when you talk about how much you can make from selling on Amazon with FBA. There is the revenue and the profit. If you have ever watched a webinar or read an article about how much people make with Amazon FBA, they often talk about the revenue. Things like, *"I made $115,000 in sales last month,"* or *"Our store generated over a million dollars last year!"*

While these numbers are meant to inspire people to start their own Amazon FBA business, they are not entirely true. Revenue is how much people paid to buy the product. This is NOT how much you are actually putting into your pocket.

There are things like the cost of inventory, brokerage fees, freight fees, inspection fees, paying contractors, and of course, Amazon has to take their cut. Now the actual profit margins (the percentage you actually make from the product after all the fees come out) can be anywhere between 10-60%.

This is a very wide range but really depends on your product and what you are spending money on. If you are buying ads, that is another expense. However, purchasing ads can drastically increase the traffic to your listing and drive sales up.

So when you are hearing people talk about how much they make from Amazon, just remember that they are generally talking about revenue. There aren't too many people out there that talk about what their profit margins are and how much they are actually putting back in their pockets.

THE ESSENTIALS OF RUNNING AMAZON ADS

It seems like every platform has their own ads. Facebook, Twitter, Google, Instagram, and now Amazon. Implementing Amazon ads can be a great tool to help grow your business much quicker. There are a few tactics that you should be aware of to help your Amazon ads gain traction from the very beginning.

- Sponsored brands help to build brand awareness

When a potential customer is searching for a product, they will be served with the sponsored ads first as they appear above the products. This will immediately help to promote brand awareness for your product. If customers are searching for similar products and your product keeps coming up, they are likely to recognize it.

- Sponsored products should use category-specific targeting

Sponsored products are slightly different than sponsored brands as they appear above, below, and along the side of the search results in Amazon. The great thing about sponsored products is that Amazon pairs your product alongside similar products within a category, which can greatly increase your chances of making a sale. You, as the advertiser, are then able to pick if your product is shown next to certain brands or other specific products. This can be extremely helpful when you are trying to target customers that already buy certain products from a certain brand. This is known as Product Attribution Targeting. This can be particularly helpful if you are selling a product that is complementary or that is an accessory to that product.

Let's take iPhones for example. If you have a product that is an iPhone accessory, like a phone case, silicone airpod cover, or dust plug, then you can choose to feature your product next to iPhones or other iPhone accessories.

When you are setting up your targeting for your Amazon ads, make sure to select manual targeting. You are able to really drill down on your target audience through selecting various attributes you would like to target, such as price range, star ratings, product categories, and brands. While Amazon might not collect as much customer information as Facebook, they have gotten pretty good at the ad game, which benefits you, the advertiser.

- Utilize negative keywords

Yes, you still need to implement SEO tactics when you are selling FBA products. But don't worry, there is a very simple explanation as to how to handle keywords and negative keywords.

Let's refer back to out iPhone example. If you are selling silicone covers for Airpods there are certain keywords that you would use. You would want to use keywords like *wireless headphones, iphone, bluetooth,* and *airpods.* You would not want to use words like *android.* Why you ask? Because people that are searching for silicone airpod covers most likely already own an iPhone and already own Airpods or are purchasing the product for someone who does.

Therefore using keywords like *android* in your ads would be a waste of money! So don't do it! Also, leave out keywords that are too general or too short, like *top* or *best.* This is only going to cost you more money in the long run. The point is that you can help to cut your advertising costs by taking advantage of negative keywords.

- Switch up your ad campaign strategies

There are two different kinds of campaigns for Amazon ads - manual and automatic. If you don't know anything about Pay Per Click (PPC) ads, there is a bit of a learning curve with this.

Automated campaigns are pretty much set and forget; however, they aren't always optimal and there is limited control. You should also be checking in on your campaigns periodically to ensure that they are still performing and you aren't wasting money. There is an advantage to using automated campaigns though. They are great for sourcing keywords to then use in your manual campaigns.

If you are new to this whole pay to play thing, then you should take the time to really learn about ads or you can outsource this. There are many freelancers and agencies available online to assist with your Pay Per Click campaigns that know all about how to optimize your ads so they keep generating sales.

Manual ads are just that, manual. These are something that you really need to keep an eye on. There is a lot that can go into manual campaigns, such as bidding on your keywords. If you don't know what you are doing you can potentially lose a lot of money. While this can sound a little scary, once you have done a few campaigns, then you will quickly become a pro at setting up and maintaining your campaigns.

Your goal with ads is to sell more and spend less. It is suggested that you use various types of Amazon ads and not just stick to one. This can help to optimize your ads, thus generating you more revenue from your ad spend.

CHAPTER SUMMARY

FBA stands for Fulfillment By Amazon. You find a product to sell, ship it to Amazon, and they handle all of the packing, shipping, returns, and customer service. FBA has the advantage of offering their customers Prime shipping.

When you start to generate revenue from your orders, you get paid your cut from Amazon every other week, which creates reliable and consistent income.

You need to keep a few key things in mind when starting your FBA business:

- Make sure you keep your products in stock.
- Consistently turn over your inventory so you don't have to pay Amazon storage fees.
- Advertise and market your FBA business.

As with any business, there are also challenges that are going to arise:

- It costs a bit more to start an FBA business.
- Amazon also requires that you pay service and fulfillment fees.

- If your inventory sits too long you can incur storage fees.
- Prime members that purchase your product might be more likely to return it.
- Amazon can be pretty picky when it comes to certain things.
- Figuring out all the tax stuff can be confusing.

While it might take a bit to get things figured out, there are also many benefits to selling through Amazon FBA:

- You save a ton of time and stress by letting Amazon fulfill your orders.
- Shipping your products from overseas is actually very affordable.
- You don't have to worry about returns and the majority of customer service.
- There is unlimited storage potential.
- Amazon can help to fulfill your orders on other platforms as well.

Choosing a product can be overwhelming; however, if you are confident in your choices and decision then you will go far! FBA is a lot of trial and error, don't get discouraged if your first product isn't a total hit. It is better to go narrower in your niche than to go wider.

FBA often starts with sourcing products from China. This allows for higher profit margins and affordable shipping. Additionally, you can modify a product to make it unique, and you don't have to travel to China to see your products.

It is advised that you establish an LLC when you are selling physical products in the case something happens to a customer and you face legal action.

Generally speaking, people make between a 10-60% profit margin on their products. There are several ways that you can help to drive more traffic to your products:

- Sponsored brands
- Category-specific targeting
- Utilize negative keywords
- Switch up your ad campaign strategies between manual and automatic

CHAPTER RESOURCES

Sourcing products

- Alibaba
- AliExpress

In the next (and last) chapter, we are going to cover everything that you need to know about selling your business for a big payout.

160

CHAPTER EIGHT
Everything You Need To Know About Selling Your Business For A Big Payout

NOW THAT WE have covered the various types of businesses that you can start and run while living your full-time dream RV life, I want to cover selling your business. There can be some major advantages to selling your business, namely a big payout and more freedom! Online businesses can be sold and bought just like traditional brick and mortar businesses.

A good example of someone selling their business for a substantial profit is J.D. Roth from Get Rich Slowly. A personal finance blog that after three years of starting it sold for 7 figures!

While this isn't going to happen with every business, it can really speak to the potential of building an online business, an asset, and selling it for a profit.

In this chapter we are going to cover how and why you should consider building a business with selling it mind. The brokerage process and what metrics you should be tracking in order to get the most out of your sale. We will also cover how long you should keep your business before you consider selling it and the best marketplaces to list your business on when selling it.

WHY YOU SHOULD BUILD A BUSINESS WITH SELLING IN MIND

One of the best things about creating an online business with the intention to sell it is that you can easily rinse and repeat the process. Starting an online business can be done with little to no money and can generate you a huge profit if you are going to sell it. Granted, some types of businesses sell for more than others and others will take more time and money to get started.

If you have started a blog, eCommerce business, publishing business, digital agency, affiliate marketing business, YouTube channel, or even freelancing, there are certain things to keep in mind when preparing to sell your business.

Even if you don't ever plan to sell your business and just implement these tactics, you will be more organized and efficient than most other business owners. You should also take into consideration that your personal circumstances can always change, like traveling full time in your RV. Wouldn't it be great to work on a business for awhile, then be able to sell it and travel around in your RV without having to worry about money?

It is always wise to build your business from the start with the intention to sell, even if you never do. This will help to put systems in place that will keep your business running smoothly with less day to day hands-on operation.

When you are ready to sell a business, potential buyers are going to want to see stats, metrics, and other important information about your business. You should be able to show potential buyers an increased profit over the previous 6-12 months. The longer a business has been profitable, the more it will sell for.

Here are the things you should be keeping track of from the very start:

- Analytics

Make sure that your website is hooked up to Google Analytics! This is especially important if you are selling a blog. Buyers want to know how much traffic that online property is getting and where it is coming from. Being able to show potential buyers your Google Analytics will help solidify your legitimacy as a real business and not that you are inflating your numbers to drive the sale price up. This also helps buyers determine potential areas of growth that they can capitalize on.

As a business owner, having analytics installed and tracking it will help you to determine your ROI. Have you been using Facebook ads to drive traffic to a landing page? Your analytics dashboard will show you if those ads are working (in addition to Facebook's own tools). It's also wise to track your analytics in a separate spreadsheet and note any significant changes. Keep track of what works so you can do more of it.

- Finances

If you haven't already set up a separate account for your business expenses and income, do it now! Not only do you need to be able to show potential buyers expenses and revenue, but you don't want to muddy things up with your personal expenses. You need to be prepared to answer questions about your monthly net revenue, gross margins, and cost of goods sold so that potential buyers can properly assess the value of your business. Overlooking the simplest thing can lose you a sale and a lot of money. If you owe money anywhere the buyer should also be aware of that, so make sure that you are paying your bills on time!

Having your finances in order is also better for you as it will help keep you organized. It is better to be fully aware of your business finances to ensure that you are actually generating revenue from the work you are putting in. You can put together a simple profit and loss statement every month using a simple spreadsheet. There are also many professional software applications for small business owners to help keep your books in order. Freshbooks and Quickbooks are two very popular and easy to use financial platforms. If the thought of bookkeeping makes you cringe, then you can outsource that too! There are many affordable accountants and freelance bookkeepers to help you with keeping your finances in order.

- Standard Operating Procedures

Standard Operating Procedures, otherwise known as SOPs, are like the manual to your business. When you are just starting out with your business it is going to take some time to figure out your processes. Once you have a system down, it's time to create SOPs for everything you do. This can be a very time consuming process, however, it will make a big difference in the sale of your business. The SOP itself is very simple. It is just a detailed document which can include bullet points, photos, screenshots, and videos on a process.

Start with a fairly simple task for your first SOP to get the hang of it. You can ensure that you have created an effective SOP, if you can hand it off to someone else and they can effectively complete the task.

Think about all the different things you do in your business. From email templates to how to properly SEO a post, you should create an SOP for everything you do. That way, when you do sell your business you can hand over your SOPs to the new owner and they will be able to run everything smoothly. SOPs also help your buyer to be able to quickly grow and scale the business rather than just getting themselves another job.

Developing SOPs for yourself can be very beneficial as well, even if you don't intend on selling your business. They are helpful for processes that you do everyday and for ones that you only do once and awhile.

For the processes that you do everyday, SOPs are helpful when you decide to outsource. Your SOP should be put together in a way that you can hand it over to someone who doesn't know your business, and they can effectively complete the task you are asking them to complete.

They are also useful for when you need to do tasks that you don't do very often as they will help to save you time. If you are not doing something everyday you aren't going to be very proficient at it. This is where SOPs are very helpful.

WHEN IS THE RIGHT TIME TO SELL YOUR BUSINESS?

This is the burning question. How long do you have to work on your business before someone is willing to pay you a good chunk of change to buy it from you? The truth is, there is no set time. There are many factors that come into determining the "right" time to sell your business. How much are you trying to make from the sale? Are you selling this business to get an influx of cash for another? What is your goal for the sale?

Before you even think about listing it for sale, you first need to have a good look at your goals and answer those questions. You can, however, get a good estimate as to how much you can sell your business with a simple valuation formula. Take your monthly net profit (your profit minus expenses) from the last six to 12 months and multiply that by a sales multiple of 20 to 60 to get your listing price. For example, a business that has a net profit of about $20,000 a month would list for around $500,000, conservatively. Realistically, it could list for anywhere between $400,000 and $1,200,000.

Notice I said list, not sell for those amounts. This is because there are always negotiations. There have been individuals who have listed their blogs for one amount and bidding wars ensued and the sale price increased to well above the listing price.

When you are considering listing your business you should audit it about six months before it is listed. Now, this does not have to be done professionally, although you could. This simply means taking a good look and fixing any issues with the business that might be unattractive to buyers. Also, during this time, you should be getting your finances, analytics, and SOPs in order for prospective buyers.

If you are working with suppliers, this can add a whole other level of complication. This can be especially important for e-commerce stores. Get your supplier to sign, in writing, that they will continue to honor the same agreement they had with you.

If you are outsourcing any of your business, that should be well documented as well. Sometimes buyers will want to outsource using their own people or they may want to keep freelancers that you are already working with as they should already know the processes.

Generally speaking, people that buy businesses like things to be as automated as possible. So try and find ways to automate and outsource any processes you can. At about three months prior to getting ready to list your business, you should make sure that everything we previously mentioned is all put together. Also make sure to read through all of your SOPs to make sure that they are all up to date and easy to understand. It is wise to get some legal help when drawing up your terms of service.

HOW TO WORK WITH A BROKER TO SELL YOUR BUSINESS

Selling a business is a lot like selling a house, you can either go at it alone or use a broker. When you are selling your business you can sell it on your own. If it is a smaller sale, potentially less than $10,000 this might be a good option. You are, however, in charge of everything when you do a private sale - finding your buyer, data transfers, and negotiations are all left up to you. If you have never made a large sale like this before, this can be rather intimidating. Furthermore, there are a lot of potential downfalls to attempting to sell your business yourself.

Your buyer reach can be drastically limited. So unless you have had people already reaching out to you about buying your business, finding buyers might be an issue. Even if you are able to find buyers, knowing whether or not they are qualified can also be another potential issue. Unfortunately, there are a lot of scammers and tire kickers out there who are going to try and lowball you, especially if they know that you are new at this.

Also, not many people out there are skilled negotiators. You have to consider that the buyer is likely to have more experience buying businesses than you have at selling them, so they might be the one taking over negotiations, and you don't want that! Finally, what about the actual aspect of actually handing everything over? Migrating a business is not a simple task and if issues arise it can become difficult for both the buyer and the seller.

So unless you know how to effectively negotiate and are comfortable migrating everything to a qualified buyer, then you should work with a broker. When you work with a broker they do all the heavy lifting for you. You don't have to worry about what information you gave to what potential buyer; nor do you have to worry about a direct competitor using the vetting process to gain access to all of your information. When you are researching brokers, you should make sure to look for one that is familiar with selling your specific type of business. While there are some similarities in all online businesses, you probably don't want to work with someone that specializes in selling blogs when you run an e-commerce store.

While there are many advantages to working with a broker, such as access to pre-qualified buyers, there are also some downsides.

It can be difficult to find good and experienced brokers as the buying and selling of online businesses is fairly new. Make sure that you are doing your research and ask for references to ensure you are not getting scammed by shady brokers who are only looking to make some money off of you. One good brokerage company to start with, if you are looking to list your business for over $50,000, is Empire Flippers, who charges a 15% commission on the sale. If you are selling a business that is going to generate under $50,000, then Flippa is another great option; they also charge a 15% commission fee.

When you have found a broker that you want to work with, there are several things that you need to put together to get the process started. you will need your traffic data, proof of your revenue and earnings, and proof that you actually own the website, domain, brand, and or trademark. It can take two to four weeks for a broker to analyze your business. After everything is ready to go, you are going to need to set your minimum sale price, this is the lowest price you are willing to go. This also helps to make sure that you aren't wasting your time with buyers who aren't serious.

Even if you decide not to sell your business and just use the tactics discussed here to run your business you will be a much more effective business owner. The more you can automate and systematize, the better.

RINSE AND REPEAT FOR MAXIMUM PROFITS

True entrepreneurs love the process of building something from scratch. When you know how to create an online business you can do it again and again. While some entrepreneurs like to keep all of their businesses and just outsource the major tasks, many also build, sell, and repeat. One thing that entrepreneurs might not be very good at though is being able to determine the fair market value for their business. This, again, is where a broker will come in handy and help you with the process. While building an online business is filled with uncertainty, working with a broker can help you to maximize your efforts and work towards a big payday.

Whether it is building simple websites to sell, e-commerce stores, or blogs, you can always rinse and repeat your process. The thing is that you always learn new things by doing this. Each business is going to be improved from the previous if you are taking each of these businesses as a learning process. You can also learn a lot from the actual sale of a business. Is there something that buyers are looking for that your other business didn't have that would have increased the sale price? If so, apply that to your next business.

WHAT TYPES OF BUSINESSES ARE BROKERS LOOKING FOR

If you have decided that you want to build a business from the ground up with the intention of selling it, here are a few types of businesses that brokers are looking for:

- Individual or packaged AdSense sites
- Sites that use Amazon Associates as the main monetization strategy
- Other affiliate sites
- Dropshipping sites
- e-Commerce stores - Shopify, WooCommerce, etc.
- Software as a Service businesses
- Sites meant to generate leads for other businesses
- Amazon FBA businesses
- Mobile apps
- A productized service, which is where freelancing becomes an actual company

And of course there are certainly sites and businesses that brokers DON'T want. These include:

- Sites and blogs that are not monetized (such as personal and journaling type blogs)
- SEO and link building service sites

- Fan based sites or those that are too similar to social media platforms
- Adult content related sites
- Gambling related sites
- Any site that promotes dubious medical claims or cures
- Anything related to criminal activity, such as hacking

So keep that in mind when you are building your business.

Brokers also look for certain things when it comes to revenue generation. Empire Flippers specifically looks for businesses that are generating at least $500 in net profit per month that is at least six-months old. When you think about it, that is not very difficult to build a business that is generating over $500 a month in net profit in six months. Especially with everything that you have learned in this book!

Once your site is listed with a broker, it's time to sit back and relax while the broker does all the heavy lifting. While some sites and businesses can sell very fast, others might take awhile to find the right buyer. Once the business has officially been sold, the broker handles the transfer of everything with minimal effort from you. While there are no guarantees that your site will sell, a good broker will continue to work with you until the right buyer is found.

In the event that you are selling a smaller site, one that is considered a "starter site," meaning that it doesn't have months or years of traffic and analytics to pull from, you still have options. Flippa is a great platform to sell newer and smaller businesses quick. These can be starter affiliate sites, ecommerce sites, and even domains. Flippa isn't really considered a broker in the traditional sense, but rather an auction site, much like eBay, but for selling businesses.

As Flippa is a marketplace rather than a broker, there are a few key factors to consider. A marketplace lets buyers and sellers communicate directly to one another. Essentially, anyone can post a website for sale and anyone can buy it. Marketplaces that sell businesses generally tend to deal with lower end sales, from $100 to tens of thousands. The great thing about marketplaces as opposed to brokers is they generally get more traffic, which means more potential buyers. This can also mean that there are a lot more people trying to sell their online assets.

If you are in the market to buy a business, a marketplace might be a good place to start. You can skip all the setup and tedious technical tasks associated with setting up a blog or ecommerce site and just buy a starter site. So for a couple hundred to a couple thousand dollars you can have someone else get things started for you.

You can also hire freelancers on sites like Fiverr and UpWork to do this as well if you want to avoid setting things up. The auction setup of a marketplace can also add value to the seller as you are able to drive up a sale price when people are actively bidding on it. When it comes to selling sites on Flippa, higher priced sites often do worse with a lower sales multiple (20x to 60x sales multiple we discussed earlier). But if you are looking for a good quality site at a lower price as a buyer this gives you an advantage.

When you are working with a broker they do they take a commission fee, but they also use things like market research and standardized valuation processes to determine a selling value. Whereas when you list or buy a business off of a marketplace, people generally don't understand sales multipliers and just pick a number that sounds good to them. There is also a lot less red tape when dealing with a market-place over a broker.

The major disadvantage of selling on Flippa or other marketplaces is the potential to get scammed, lose all your site's info, and all of your money. While no system is perfect, finding a reputable broker will drastically reduce your chances of getting scammed.

CHAPTER SUMMARY

Building a business is so much more than bringing in income, you are building an asset. Once you know what you are doing you can easily rinse and repeat the process of building and selling businesses. You can implement these tactics to become a more effective and efficient business owner.

Potential buyers will want to see:

- Analytics
- An increase in profits over the last 6-12 months
- Finances
- Systems and standard operating procedures

Generally speaking, you should be generating a positive revenue for six to 12 months before selling a business. You can easily come up with a valuation for your business by taking the monthly net profit and applying a sales multiple of 20-60.

Working with a broker can make the whole process a lot smoother and easier.

Types of businesses that sell well:

- Individual or packaged AdSense sites
- Sites that use Amazon Associates as the main monetization strategy
- Other affiliate sites
- Dropshipping sites
- e-Commerce stores - Shopify, WooCommerce, etc.
- Software as a Service businesses
- Sites meant to generate leads for other businesses
- Amazon FBA businesses
- Mobile apps
- A productized service, which is where freelancing becomes an actual company

CHAPTER RESOURCES

Bookkeeping

- Freshbooks
- Quickbooks

Listing your business for sale

- Empire Flippers
- Flippa

FINAL WORDS

WE COVERED A lot in this book, and I realize that it can be overwhelming.

I hope that you realize by now that you don't have to stay stuck in your 9-5 job working for someone else to help them live their dreams. You can work for yourself and have all the freedom that you choose in order to live full-time in your RV on your terms.

Whether or not you already own your dream RV, whether or not you have started a business before or are completely new to these processes, it doesn't matter. You have it in you to achieve your dream life. People are doing it every day, don't get left behind!

It is entirely possible to live your full-time RV life while making a really good income online.

You can make a full-time income with part-time work as a freelancer, blogger, YouTuber, online publisher, affiliate marketer, Amazon FBA, or by selling your business. While it won't necessarily take a lot of money to get started, it is going to take a lot of time and dedication to get going.

- Want to become a freelancer, start looking on the job boards.
- Want to be a blogger, then figure out what you want to blog about and buy a domain and hosting.
- Grab your phone and start recording your first YouTube video.
- Hit that publish button on Amazon and list your first book.
- Start posting those affiliate links.
- Pick a product to sell.
- Then sell your business and rinse and repeat the process again and again!

Now I have given you a lot of information to go out and get started, but it's up to you. You are the only one that is going to make you successful. You can read all the best books, listen to all the best podcasts, watch all the videos, and read all the blogs, but it won't matter unless you are taking action!

Remember, progress is better than perfection. You are going to mess up. You are going to fail, maybe even more than once. You are going to beat your head against the wall a couple of times.

If you want to live your full-time RV life, you have to work for it. No one is going to hand it over to you!

You determine your success. You determine how much work you are willing to put in to achieve your dream. I can't do it for you.

So what are you waiting for?

RESOURCES

Awosika, A. (2019, July 17). Kindle Direct Publishing: How to Make Real Money on Amazon. Retrieved July 21, 2019, from https://smartblogger.com/kindle-publishing/

Barbara. (2019). YouTube Creator Academy: Making advertiser-friendly content [YouTube]. Retrieved July 28, 2019, from https://creatoracademy.youtube.com/page/lesson/advertiser-friendly?cid=earn-money&hl=en

Berger, B. (2017, March 29). 5 Ways to Automate Your Freelance Business. Retrieved July 26, 2019, from https://freelancetofreedomproject.com/5-ways-automate-freelance-business/

Bryant, D. (2014). How to Find the Perfect Product to Import from China and Sell On Amazon | EcomCrew. Retrieved August 2, 2019, from https://www.ecomcrew.com/8-secrets-to-picking-the-perfect-product-to-wholesale-from-china/

Bryant, David. (2018). How to Import from China in 2019 | EcomCrew. Retrieved August 3, 2019, from https://www.ecomcrew.com/how-to-import-from-china/

Carragher, G. (2018, December 13). Chapter 12 How to Leverage the Power of Amazon FBA. Retrieved July 31, 2019, from https://www.bigcommerce.com/blog/amazon-fba/

Carrell, P. (2019, June 25). The Ultimate Guide to The Amazon Associates Program. Retrieved July 31, 2019, from https://www.authorityhacker.com/amazon-associates/

Chesson, D. (2019a, March 15). How To Make An Audiobook: Publishing on ACX and Audiobook Marketing. Retrieved July 23, 2019, from https://kindlepreneur.com/how-to-make-an-audiobook/

Chesson, D. (2019b, July 22). Smashwords vs Draft2Digital vs PublishDrive Review. Retrieved July 23, 2019, from https://kindlepreneur.com/smashwords-vs-draft2digital/

Chesson, D. (2017, December 21). Kindle Select vs KU vs Mass Publication: What's an Author to Do? Retrieved July 23, 2019, from https://kindlepreneur.com/e4-kindle-select-vs-ku-vs-other-markets/

Chesson, D. (2019c, June 27). Book Cover Design Mastery. Retrieved July 22, 2019, from https://kindlepreneur.com/book-cover-design/

Cooke, J. (2013, December 16). Selling Websites Made Easy – How to Sell Your Site With Us - Empire Flippers. Retrieved August 4, 2019, from https://empireflippers.com/how-to-sell-my-website/

Edwards, G. (2018, July 17). Top 10 Affiliate Networks and Programs That Aren't Amazon in 2019 - Empire Flippers. Retrieved July 31, 2019, from https://empireflippers.com/best-affiliate-networks-programs/

Elaine, K. (2019). YouTube Creator Academy: Building Your Audience [YouTube]. Retrieved July 28, 2019, from https://creatoracademy.youtube.com/page/lesson/build-a-sustainable-community?cid=fans

Fiverr. (2019). Fiverr Homepage. Retrieved July 24, 2019, from https://fiverr.com/start-selling

Flynn, P. (2018, October 24). Five Truths About the Mindset of a Successful Entrepreneur. Retrieved July 20, 2019, from https://www.smartpassiveincome.com/mindset-of-a-successful-entrepreneur/

Hogan, C. (2019, March 4). What Is Passive Income and How Do I Build It? Retrieved July 20, 2019, from https://www.daveramsey.com/blog/what-is-passive-income

James, S. (2017, December 14). Are You A Dabbler? Retrieved July 20, 2019, from https://projectlife-mastery.com/are-you-a-dabbler/

Kniep, S. (2017, October 9). The mindset you MUST have if you want to build passive income | Just One Dime Blog. Retrieved July 20, 2019, from https://justonedime.com/blog/the-mindset-you-must-have-if-you-want-to-build-your-passive-income

Masters, J. (2019, May 24). Selling a Blog for 7 Figures after 3 years of Starting it with JD Roth - Eventual Millionaire. Retrieved August 5, 2019, from https://eventualmillionaire.com/jd-roth/

Mijatovic, B. (2017, November 2). How to Prepare and Sell Your Online Business - Empire Flippers. Retrieved August 4, 2019, from https://empire-flippers.com/prepare-sell-online-business/

Miller, L. (2018, May 23). 7 Myths About Passive Income You Can't Afford to Believe. Retrieved August 4, 2019, from https://www.entrepreneur.com/article/313137

Morrow, J. (2019, June 7). How to Make Money Blogging (Free Guide for 2019). Retrieved July 27, 2019, from https://smartblogger.com/make-money-blogging/

Muller, B. (2019, July 12). SEO 101: Why is it important? – Beginner's Guide to SEO. Retrieved July 27, 2019, from https://moz.com/beginners-guide-to-seo/why-search-engine-marketing-is-necessary

Patel, N. (2019, February 15). Affiliate Marketing Made Simple: A Step-by-Step Guide. Retrieved July 30, 2019, from https://neilpatel.com/what-is-affiliate-marketing/

Perkins, G. (2018, July 31). How to Start a Youtube Channel: Step-by-Step for Beginners [YouTube]. Retrieved July 27, 2019, from https://www.youtube.com/watch?v=AE6M3hcHnyw

Perez, S. (2018, June 22). YouTube introduces channel memberships, merchandise and premieres. Retrieved July 28, 2019, from https://techcrunch.com/2018/06/21/youtube-introduces-chan-nel-memberships-merchandise-and-premieres/

Ramirez, V. (2018, February 11). Guide: How I Made $7,645 Part-time On UpWork in Less than 2 Months. Retrieved July 24, 2019, from https://www.isvicto-rious.com/upwork-freelancing-guide/

Sameera. (2019). YouTube Creator Academy: Ads on YouTube [YouTube]. Retrieved July 28, 2019, from https://creatoracademy.youtube.com/page/lesson/ad-types?cid=earn-money

Sell My Site. (2018, June 13). Ultimate Guide to Buying & Selling on Flippa. Retrieved August 4, 2019, from https://sellmysite.com/buy-sell-flippa/

Skrba, A. (2018, April 8). What is a Blog? - Explanation of Terms Blog, Blogging & Blogger (2019). Retrieved July 26, 2019, from https://firstsite-guide.com/what-is-blog/

Stephen. (2019). YouTube Creator Academy: Make Money on YouTube [YouTube]. Retrieved July 28, 2019, from https://creatoracademy.youtube.com/page/lesson/revenue-basics

Swinunski, M. (2019, March 25). Build, Grow, Sell, and Repeat. - Empire Flippers. Retrieved August 4, 2019, from https://empireflippers.com/build-grow-sell-and-repeat/

Valentine, M. (2018, May 4). How to Start a Successful YouTube Channel in this Day and Age | Goalcast. Retrieved July 27, 2019, from https://www.goalcast.com/2018/03/06/how-to-start-a-youtube-channel/

Wordstream. (2019, May 1). 8 Advanced Tips for Advertising on Amazon. Retrieved August 5, 2019, from https://www.wordstream.com/blog/ws/2019/05/01/amazon-advertising-tips